THERE IS NO SECOND

America by Steven Dews

THERE IS NO SECOND

The definitive account of the first race in 1851 for what would become 'America's Cup'

MAGNUS WHEATLEY

The America's Cup, Barcelona, 2024.

Dedicated to Clare & Harry

Published by Seahorse Publishers Ltd., 1 Langley Court, Pyle Street, Newport,
Isle of Wight PO30 1LA

ISBN 978-1-3999-8328-0

A CIP catalogue record for this book is available from the British Library.

Cover painting:	*America* by Steven Dews, with thanks to the artist and David Roe of Rosenstiels. Steven Dews limited edition prints available from www.printsandfineart.com
Foreword:	SailingShots by Maria Muiña / America's Cup Archive
Introduction:	Ben Wood / PPL
Postscript:	Emirates Team New Zealand / America's Cup Archive *p176* Ian Roman / America's Cup Archive *p179*

Illustration and photographic credits: *pp184–185*

Printed and bound by CPI Group (UK) Ltd, Croydon, CR0 4YY

CONTENTS

Grant Dalton, CEO Emirates Team New Zealand.

FOREWORD

The greatest phrase in the America's Cup and the one that sums it all up is 'There is no second'. When you win, you win it all. Such is the unique nature of this competition, still rooted as it is in parts in the Deed of Gift, the document that originated in 1857 when George L. Schuyler gifted 'America's Cup' to the New York Yacht Club.

Unlike many sports, where there are governing bodies and entities sitting above and dictating the course of the sport into the future, the America's Cup is unique. Here it is the winner who becomes the sole arbiter, holder and defender, ultimately the one who can drive its direction, rules, venue, date and vessel.

The key tenet of the America's Cup, as written in the original Deed of Gift, is that it is 'perpetually a challenge cup for friendly competition between foreign countries'. This may well have been true and the intention when the Deed was written in 1857, but it's not the case anymore and it hasn't been for a long time. Today, it's a hard-fought battle from the beginning to the very end of every campaign, and with so many variables, it remains one of the hardest feats in sport to either win or defend.

Only four countries in the 173-year history of the competition have held the America's Cup – America, Australia, New Zealand and Switzerland. Vast fortunes and effort have been spent on winning the trophy, and it sits, quite rightly, at the apex of sport, very much as the Mount Everest of sailing. It's no secret that the Defender has an advantage, but in the modern era, with multiple challengers emerging, the role of the Challenger of Record, the syndicate whose challenge is the first accepted, works closely with the Defender to define the protocol and rules of engagement for the next event, giving them a top table seat and a real chance to steal a march.

Looking back through the history of the America's Cup, from the very first race around the Isle of Wight in 1851 to the first challenge in 1870, the era so lavishly researched and described in this book, you will come away perhaps with the undeniable notion that advancement in technology always wins. Experience, and indeed history, shows that the fastest boat aligned with the best overall programme and the very best people is the one that almost always emerges victorious.

America sailed to Great Britain across the Atlantic not only with a design based on the East Coast pilot boats but with very different, flat-cut sails that allowed it to go to windward better. Through the early 20th century and into the 1930s and the J Class era, technology abounded with radical reinvention and advancement of sailing by designers such as Nathaniel Herreshoff, Starling Burgess and Olin Stephens. The 12-Metre era saw the challengers get closer and closer to the Americans until, in 1983, *Australia II* ended the New York Yacht Club's 132-year winning streak with a winged keel, great sailing, an outstanding sail design programme and a real 'team' ethos.

The International America's Cup Class (IACC) was introduced in the early 1990s as an antidote to what was known as a 'Deed of Gift challenge' by New Zealand in 1988, and saw technology again take centre stage. As the class evolved, so too did the whole industry around the America's Cup, and indeed yachting itself with many and varied technologies trickling down to the grass roots of the sport. Where the America's Cup went, the sport of sailing followed. By 2013, as giant catamarans began to get up on foils and 'fly' out of the water, the biggest revolution in the sport of sailing came into the mainstream and this was adapted and acknowledged to where we are today with extraordinary foiling monohulls.

Nobody enters the Cup to lose – it's too difficult and it's too expensive. It takes everything you have and more with teams bringing in vast internal and external resources in engineering, hydro and aerodynamics, artificial intelligence, mechatronics, simulation, pure naval architecture, systems engineering and computer analysis, all to find an edge in boatspeed. Little is left to chance.

A crucial element of the modern era is the development of new pathways created through the Youth and inaugural Women's America's Cup events. To facilitate and herald a new dawn, Emirates Team New Zealand's Design Office came out with the AC40 – World Sailing's Boat of the Year in 2023 – a foiling, battery-powered 40-foot version of the AC75 capable of astonishing speeds under the control of a crew of four with two helms and two trimmers. This will give the next generation an opportunity to race at the highest level and the chance, afforded by the America's Cup, to shine on the global stage. The stars of tomorrow will all be competing and the winners will define the future of the event and write their own page in history.

My view is that the America's Cup has never been in ruder health. The challenge remains the same and it is arguably the hardest competition in international sports to win. The team that does so brings every element together in terms of personnel, technology and competitiveness, all into one thrilling crescendo of sporting excellence.

To truly understand the America's Cup, it is important to understand its past. What you will learn here in this book is the origin story of this competition with its socio-political backdrop as well as some truly astounding facts, and challenges to accepted wisdom. Some of these have never been revealed or questioned before. The name of the 'Signal-Master', so long thought to have been lost in history, who was likely to have uttered the phrase to Queen Victoria, 'Ma'am there is no second' is revealed. The story of the uncovering is a fascinating piece of investigative journalism by an author who has had a lifelong fascination with the America's Cup. His enthusiasm for the competition is infectious.

Magnus Wheatley's book is a must-read for anyone wanting to immerse themselves in the history of this great event and to understand how it has become the pinnacle of the sailing world.

Good reading!

Grant Dalton
March 2024

Magnus Wheatley at the National Archives, Kew.

INTRODUCTION

When I was 11 years old, the America's Cup came into my life – or to be more precise, on 26 September 1983, it not so much came as burst into my conscious with *Australia II*'s defeat of the American yacht *Liberty*, skippered by Dennis Conner. The following day, the likes of Barry Pickthall, Bob Fisher and David Miller, writing for the great British newspapers, brought breathless commentary to life as they told of the end of the longest winning streak in sports history. Fuzzy, print-heavy snaps of the Australian yacht, skippered by John Bertrand, rounding up on the *Black Knight* finishing vessel of the New York Yacht Club demanded further investigation and query.

This was satisfied by Bertrand's first-hand account of this achievement in *Born to Win* (1985), which today still ranks as one of the all-time greatest reads on winning the America's Cup. Conner's book *No Excuse to Lose* (1978) further fuelled the fire of knowledge, and later the imagination was sparked by both his tome *Comeback* (1987) and that captivating February 1987 *Time* front cover of the deeply tanned, mercurial genius holding the wheel of what was then the greatest yacht in the world. Conner was, of course, the first to lose and then regain the Cup, and that underdog spirit absolutely resonated.

By then, I found myself catching the early train to school in Southampton with a most treasured possession (I still have it today): namely a lever arch file where I studiously documented every race of that wonderful regatta in Perth, Western Australia, in 1987. With little regard for fellow readers or the librarian, I cut out every article from *The Times*, *Telegraph* and *Guardian* to create my own personal 'blog' project, long before such a thing was a thing – I apologise.

There I left it and pursued a career, whilst keeping a watchful, interested, somewhat jealous eye on the America's Cup from a distance as it pinged back to America and then to New Zealand – my favourite country in the world. But finally, a chance meeting with the then sports editor of the *Financial Times* in London presented an opportunity to cover the Cup. I took it gleefully and so began the long road to forging a new career fuelled by my passion for this contest and its long history.

I am lucky to have worked for great editors in the media covering the event and have worked too on the other side of the fence for teams. Today, I am extremely fortunate to be working for the America's Cup, covering the daily recon as well as the event itself for the organisers. The boats may have changed, but the human and technological stories are still abundant. It was ever thus, and the contest promises as always to be a pinnacle event on the global sporting calendar and certainly the apex event of sailing.

The genesis for this book has been a long time in the making, but was fired by a brief discussion with Grant Dalton after I wrote the history of the first race in 1851 for the America's Cup website. A comment about the detail, unbeknown to Grant despite his long participation in the America's Cup, made me want to go in deeper than has ever been done before, in more detail, and, most crucially, back to the sources. Where this book took me was to uncomfortable truths, outright untruths, plenty of rehashing in respected sources and the backdrop of a self-serving and disorganised media, which has enabled me to draw conclusions that challenge, quite profoundly, the received and accepted version of events.

The highlight, which still gives me goosebumps to this day, was the uncovering at the National Archives in Kew, London, of the names of the Yeoman of the Signals onboard the *Victoria & Albert* yacht in 1851. To many, the tale of Her Majesty Queen Victoria being told by a 'signal-master' that, 'Ma'am, there is no second', when she enquired as to the standings in the race around the Isle of Wight, whilst at anchor in Alum Bay, is easily and conveniently cast aside as 'apocryphal', or simply something that could not have happened. It was certainly possible and, whatever the truth, if it was said by a signal-master onboard the yacht that day, then this book reveals the likely names – never before associated with the America's Cup.

What started out as a peer into early Victorian Britain, its curiosities, its cultivation of sporting events and rampant, ingrained betting, became something so much more. You hear a lot of authors saying that where they finished is not where they intended or what they planned. This book was no different as the stories and the characters engrossed and the detail fascinated. It has been a pleasure to research and write, something which, in the spirit of the America's Cup, has been totally all-consuming to the point of fanatical.

One question asked by relatives is 'I know you're interested in the history of the America's Cup, but will anyone else be?' And it's a great question. Primarily, I wrote it because I love the story of how the original 'RYS £100 Cup' came to be 'America's Cup', and for anyone looking for an at-source version of events, with an interest in this great and unique sporting competition, it is hopefully compelling. The socio-political ramifications of the involvement of Queen Victoria, amidst the hostility shown towards Americans at the time, makes this as fascinating a read for the more casual observer of one of the greatest sporting feats in history.

One of the observations along the 'journey' has been how this history has been distorted to suit a narrative, a true example of how many histories are rehashed, repackaged, represented and told. Therefore, at every juncture I have made all efforts to find the source and present it in the manner in which it was originally intended. You may find some parts challenge what you *knew* already but hopefully within a context that broadens the understanding around the first race for what would become America's Cup after its gifting to the New York Yacht Club in 1857. The first challenge of James Lloyd Ashbury in 1870 felt like the appropriate place to put a full stop – partly because the Cup's format changed so much thereafter, going from fleet to one-on-one match races.

It's a compelling story with almost unbelievable, other-worldly characters and a lingering sense of intrigue befitting what some regard as the Holy Grail of sailing and one of the truly great endeavours in world sport where today, just as in 1851, 'There is no second'.

Magnus Wheatley
March 2024

Henry William Paget, 1st Marquess of Anglesey KG, GCB, GCH, PC (1768–1854).

CHAPTER ONE

THE MARQUESS OF ANGLESEY

Here lies the Marquis of Anglesey's limb.
The Devil will have the remainder of him.[1]

Any historical account charting the America's Cup must begin with the formation of The Yacht Club in 1815 and the influence of Henry William Paget, a devout sea-dog and great war-leader, who would eventually become the 1st Marquess of Anglesey following his considerable heroics at the Battle of Waterloo. It was Anglesey who not only bought and donated what would become 'America's Cup' but arguably saved yacht racing in Cowes and the fate of the Royal Yacht Squadron.

The Old Thatched House Tavern, or 'Thatch'd House', as detailed by the satirist Jonathan Swift, was situated at number 74 on the then literary and artistic street of St James's, in the heart of London, where Sir Christopher Wren died in 1723 and Lord Byron lodged in 1811. With its vast public rooms, it was the clubland venue, of some two centuries standing, where the great universities and Britain's foremost public schools held meetings, along with nascent London art societies.

The Royal Naval Club also met at the tavern, and by the early 19th century, St James's Street had become a fashionable and cultural thoroughfare. Surrounded by Turkish bath houses, some of which dated back to 1699, coffee shops, chocolate houses and the foreign and domestic news house of

[1] Satirical graffiti added to the tombstone of the Marquess of Angelsey's amputated leg in the village of Waterloo. Note the French spelling of 'Marquess' as 'Marquis'.

the *Tatler*, a foremost society magazine that chronicled the great and the good, it could be argued that 'The Thatch'd' was at its epicentre.

To number 74 St James's Street, on the 1 June 1815, arrived the founding members of what would become 'The Yacht Club' for gentlemen interested in salt-water yachting. No commodore was appointed, nor flag-officers at this initial meeting, with the first Commodore, the Earl of Yarborough, coming much later in the 1820s, but an agreement was made between the members at the 'Thatch'd' to meet twice a year – once in London and once on the Isle of Wight, initially at East Cowes at either the Medina Hotel or the Vine Inn and merely to converse about their mutual interest.

Lord Grantham chaired the meeting and both a treasurer in East Cowes and an alternative in London were appointed. An 11-point agenda was agreed between the 42 original members with stipulations for membership, costs to join and details of the two meetings, also that a minimum limit of sailing vessels of ten tons be adopted to become eligible for membership. Interestingly, Lord Grantham is still remembered today at the Royal Yacht Squadron by way of a bronze mermaid sculpture modelled on the Olympic swimmer Sharron Davies which sits looking out to the Cowes harbour entrance from the rocks that form the outer breakwater of the club's harbour. Grantham's yacht was called *Mermaid*.

The Yacht Club was by no means the first club to organise sailboat racing: the Cumberland Society had been founded in 1775 after the Duke of Cumberland sponsored a race between Westminster and Putney for a nominal silver cup and the Society was organising a form of racing on the Thames. The *Badminton Library of Sports and Pastimes* suggests that the 'Cumberland Fleet', with the Royal Thames Yacht Club its lineal descendant, may with all justice claim the title of the 'Mother of Yacht-Racing', at least in Great Britain.

And it goes on to describe those first races:

> The year 1770 was a most important epoch in Thames yachting. The 'King's Fisher' was clinker built and her owner, Commodore Thomas Taylor of the Cumberland Fleet, was so thoroughly the practical founder of yacht racing on the Thames that his statue should be placed on the Thames Embankment – with a bronze plaque of his yacht and the cups he won – and if times are too bad to go that length, a medallion portrait plaque could go on the Temple Embankment Arch, for the

> 'King's Fisher' was built close by … In the year of grace 1775 the first rowing regatta that was ever held in England took place upon the Thames – on June 23.

Previously to this, however, a meeting of 'several very respectable gentlemen, proprietors of sailing vessels and pleasure boats on the river,' held their annual meeting at Battersea, and resolved that on the regatta day they would draw up in a line opposite Ranelagh Gardens, so as not to be in the way of the competing rowing boats. On July 6 of the same year an advertisement appears in the *Advertiser*, that his Royal Highness Henry Frederick, Duke of Cumberland (a brother of George III, and an admiral in the British Navy) was about to give a silver cup to be sailed for on July 11. The advertisement was as follows:

> A Silver Cup, the gift of His Royal Highness the Duke of Cumberland, is to be sailed for on Tuesday, the 11th instant, from Westminster Bridge to Putney Bridge and back, by Pleasure Sailing Boats, from two to five tons burthen, and constantly lying above London Bridge. Any gentleman inclined to enter his Boat may be informed of particulars by applying to Mr. Roberts, Boat-builder, Lambeth, any time before Saturday Noon next.

On account of the weather, however, the race was postponed until 13 July, when it came off with great success, and the *Aurora*, owned by a Mr Parkes, described as 'late of Ludgate Hill', won the cup. The second boat in was named the *Fly*, but who owned her the newspapers of the day forgot to mention. From the *Morning Post* we get the information that only those boats 'which were never let out to hire' would be allowed to enter, and also that 'the Gentlemen, about 18 or 20 in number, who sail for the prize have come to a resolution to be dressed in aquatic uniforms'. This seems to prove that the club had already been formed before the match and was probably an outcome of the club at Battersea mentioned above. We also find from the old newspapers that the owners (who, by the way, were always styled 'captain') had to steer their respective vessels, and in the case of this first match were allowed two assistants; so it would seem that what nowadays are called 'Corinthian rules' were in the early period of yacht-racing a *sine qua non*.

Even before that, it is known that The Water Club of Cork organised 'manoeuvres' and signalling between pilot and revenue cutters where a 'prodigal expenditure of gunpowder' was the norm (according to writings at the National Maritime Museum). Whilst dotted along the south-coast of

England from Plymouth to Weymouth and on to Portsmouth and Cowes, fisherman, pilot boats and Royal Navy cutters would often compete. Today there is still record of a Royal Naval regatta off Cowes in 1776.

Indeed, there is some confusion as to whether the 'The Yacht Club' was actually established in 1815 as a club seal dates a possible formation of association as early as 1812. Certainly though, articles of membership, rules and fees came into force post the 1815 meeting so that is arguably the starting point for the club. Furthermore, it is almost certain that the club was the first to use the word 'Yacht' in its title, and although the numbers that were present at that original meeting in 1815 were not recorded (ten were required at a minimum), one notable founder member, the 2nd Earl of Uxbridge, Henry William Paget, was almost certainly not present.

The Battle of Waterloo was just 17 days away and Paget had been drafted in by the Duke of Wellington to command the 13,000-strong allied cavalry and some 44 horse artillery batteries. As the Earl of Uxbridge between 1812 and 1815, Paget had a distinguished war record. After serving as a member of parliament for Carnarvon and then for Milborne Port, he took part in the Flanders Campaign in the mid-1790s and then commanded the cavalry for Sir John Moore's army in Spain during the Peninsular War from 1807–1814.

The deciding defeat of Napoleon in the United Kingdom of the Netherlands (now in Belgium) on the 18 June 1815 was instructed by the Seventh Coalition comprising the Anglo-allied forces led by the Duke of Wellington and three corps of the Prussian armies led by Field Marshall Gebhard Leberecht von Blücher. A notable charge saw Paget lead some 2,000 troops of the British heavy cavalry against the French Corps columns of the Comte d'Erlon, sending the French infantry away in complete disorder. Paget's troops continued in pursuit and were ambushed by the French cavalry's counterattack, and he spent the rest of the battle leading a series of intense charges against the French, reportedly losing a number of horses that were shot from under him.

Towards the closing moments of the battle, as the French cannon-fire diminished, the Duke of Wellington took out his field telescope and was surveying the battlefield when one of the last of the French grapeshot flew past Wellington and into Paget's right knee, shattering it completely. Turning to the Duke of Wellington, Paget is supposed to have exclaimed, 'By God, sir, I've lost my leg!', to which the Duke replied, 'By God, sir, so you have!'.

Paget was carried from the battlefield and taken to his headquarters in the village of Waterloo, to a house owned by Monsieur Hyacinthe Joseph Marie Paris. The doctor inspected his leg and found that the head of the tibia was fractured, the outer hamstring severed, and the capsular ligament filled with fragments of bone and cartilage. He informed Paget that his leg would have to be amputated. Remarkably the doctor also noted that 'his pulse was calm and regular as if he had just risen from his bed in the morning and he displayed no expression of uneasiness though his suffering must have been extreme.'

Paget was seated in a wooden chair for the operation and was provided with no anaesthesia, enduring the amputation by saw with barely a sound, except at one point when he remarked that the blade did not seem very sharp. Once it had been removed, Monsieur Paris requested whether he could have the severed leg so that he could bury it in his garden. Upon receiving permission, Paris placed the leg in a small wooden coffin and buried it under a willow tree. A small tombstone was erected over it carrying an inscription which read:

> Here lies the leg of the illustrious and valiant Earl Uxbridge, Lieutenant-General of His Britannic Majesty, Commander in Chief of the English, Belgian and Dutch cavalry, wounded on the 18 June 1815 at the memorable battle of Waterloo, who, by his heroism, assisted in the triumph of the cause of mankind, gloriously decided by the resounding victory of the said day.

Surprisingly, the burial site became an attraction for European High Society with records of the King of Prussia and the Prince of Orange visiting. The Prince Regent is said to have wept almost uncontrollably when he read the inscription, but equally there were dissenting voices elucidated by an inscription mischievously scrawled on the concrete tombstone that read: 'Here lies the Marquis of Anglesey's limb. The Devil will have the remainder of him.'

Whilst the Battle of Waterloo effectively ended Paget's active military career, it did not diminish his place in society. Having assumed the title of 2nd Earl of Uxbridge after his father's death in 1812, he was appointed a Knight Grand Cross of the Order of the Bath in January 1815, and on 4 July 1815, just over two weeks after Waterloo, the Prince Regent afforded the title of 1st Marquess of Anglesey. A 27-metre-tall Doric memorial column, the Anglesey Column, was erected in Llanfairpwllgwyngyll, near the Menai Strait in Wales, two years after the Battle of Waterloo, to commemorate his valour in the Napoleonic Wars. He went on to become a field marshal and Knight of the Garter, twice serving as Lord Lieutenant of Ireland, and twice as Master-General of the Ordnance. Later in 1831, he became the first Commodore of the Royal Irish Yacht Club in Kingstown, now known more familiarly as Dun Laoghaire, and his connection with the sea was a life-long passion.

Advances in prosthetics in the early 1800s facilitated the Marquess of Anglesey's mobility, but it was to the fabled James Potts of Chelsea, London's premier artificial limb-maker that the Marquess turned to develop something quite extraordinary for the time. Paget's wooden leg was hollowed out to make it lighter and with an articulated knee, ankle and toe joints, he was able to walk almost naturally, whilst the use of catgut tendons offered smooth and nearly soundless flexion of the joints. The design was such an improvement over existing artificial legs that Potts applied for a patent on the design with the name 'Anglesey leg'.

As the 1820s arrived, The Yacht Club was benefitting from a boom in popularity, prompted in part by the Prince Regent's joining in 1817. When he acceded to the throne as King George IV in 1820, the club's connection with royalty was secured when it applied for, and was granted, the new name of 'The Royal Yacht Club'.

The Duke of Clarence and the Duke of Gloucester joined the club in 1821 whilst the original rules were amended to require ownership of yachts of over 20 tons for prospective members to apply. The club had actively supported the Cowes Regatta in 1818, with a purse of some £70 for the competing local boatmen, before assuming its running soon after. Cowes then became the Solent's central hub of yachting, signalling and, increasingly, racing.

In 1815 a race between Joseph Weld's 60-ton cutter *Charlotte* and Thomas Assheton Smith's 65-ton cutter *Elizabeth* was said to have attracted betting slips of up to 2,000 guineas on its outcome – an enormous sum for the time, with large crowds witnessing the entertainment; the *Charlotte* won and the not inconsiderable sum of £500 was secured. In 1819, the Marquess of Anglesey bested a fleet containing vessels owned by Joseph Weld and William Baring for a sweepstake of £150 with additional winning of some £800 being secured on the outcome through side betting.

Buying further into the boom, the Marquess of Anglesey commissioned Philip Sainty of Wivenhoe, builder of the fastest smuggling ships in the land, to build what would become the 113-ton cutter, the *Pearl*. The Marquess's interest in technological innovation, it could be argued, had already been proven by the design of the famed 'Anglesey leg' and his competitive, and showman-like, approach to yacht racing was deeply ingrained. As he was quoted saying, 'I had ever a passion for the Navy at Westminster; every shilling I had went in boat hire.'

However, a fascinating scenario occurred when Anglesey originally tried to make contact with Sainty and found that he was languishing at His Majesty's pleasure at Springfield jail, now HMP Chelmsford, under a smuggling related offence. In order to get the best boatbuilder to construct what he hoped would be a winning vessel, Anglesey had to secure a King's pardon not only for Sainty but also for his brother and brother-in-law who were languishing in Maidstone jail on similar charges. With his high-society connections, the pardons were granted.

By June 1820, the *Pearl* was launched, and by the following summer she was winning races beating William Baring's *Hussar* with yacht racing and trials of speed very much front and centre. In July 1825, it is recorded that Joseph and James Weld challenged Anglesey to a two-part match between their dominant boat *Arrow* and the Marquess's *Pearl* for £500 plus another race for £300 between the Weld's 43-ton *Julia* and Anglesey's 42-ton *Liberty*. Ahead of the two-day double-header, the Marquess is said to have publicly commented: 'If the *Pearl* be beaten, I will burn her as soon as we get back.' He won in controversial circumstances, winning the first race out to a marker boat in Swanage Bay and back by what records simply recount as a 'fluke' with no further details. He lost the second day, the *Pearl* was saved from the furnace, but the remark was an indication of the colourful, sporting controversy that Henry William Paget seemed to garner throughout his decorated life.

Perhaps what sealed the Marquess of Anglesey's reputation in society was his support for the proceedings against Queen Caroline, the estranged wife of the future King George IV whom he had married in 1795, and who was accused of infidelity but remained popular with the public. When George became King in January 1820, Caroline had returned from a form of self-imposed exile in Italy to stake her claim as Queen Consort, but the King who had demanded, and been denied, a divorce, barred her from attending his coronation in July 1821 and she died in London three weeks later.

Indeed, the Marquess of Anglesey's life had been one of controversy even outside of politics and royal matters. Having married Lady Caroline Elizabeth Villiers, the daughter of George Villiers, the 4th Earl of Jersey in 1795, the couple went on to have eight children. However, after his scandalous elopement with Lady Charlotte Cadogan, daughter of Charles Cadogan, the 1st Earl of Cadogan, such was the scandal that Charlotte's brother Henry challenged Lord Paget, as he was then styled, to a pistol duel saying:

> My Lord, I hereby request you to name a time and place where I may meet you, to obtain satisfaction for the injury done to myself and my whole family by your conduct to my sister. I have to add that the time must be as early as possible, and the place not in the immediate neighbourhood of London, as it is by concealment alone that I am able to evade the Police.

The duel was arranged for Wimbledon Common and, by accounts, both men discharged their pistols with no harm coming to either, but honour was satisfied. Caroline divorced Paget on the 29 November 1810, according to public record, and he married Lady Charlotte soon afterwards and went on, remarkably, to have a further ten children with her.

Most notably, and pertinently to yachting, in 1826, the Marquess of Anglesey assumed the role of captain of Cowes Castle as a sinecure, receiving a stipend for the honour and overseeing not only its running as a military garrison consisting of the captain, a porter, two soldiers, a master gunner and five regular gunners but also some lavish improvements to what would become a holiday home for the Marquess through the summer months, the key yachting period in Cowes.

The Royal Yacht Club, which had originally met on the 7 August 1815 at the Royal Medina Hotel in East Cowes, now the site of the Wight Shipyard Co., was still based out of the Gloster Hotel on the Cowes Parade. It wasn't until after the Marquess of Anglesey's death in 1854, and the subsequent passing of the lease by the government to his son-in-law Lord Conyngham, that thoughts of the club moving to the premises were mooted.

By 1855, the Royal Yacht Club took charge of the property on a lease (they wouldn't assume the head title from the Crown until 1917) and instructed the architect Anthony Salvin to make major renovations including the northwest turret, gatehouse, serving wing and platform plus upgraded lodgings for members over a two-year period to 1858.

Charles Anderson-Pelham, the 2nd Baron Yarborough and later the first Earl of Yarborough had stewarded the club in his role as its first Commodore with great grace, steering it through difficult times when the yacht racing became fraught – particularly in racing off Cowes in 1829, which proved to be a tricky time when the first handicapping systems were introduced. He also put great stock on the development of the complex creation of signalling. Any reference to what is now the Royal Yacht Squadron is deeply rooted in the application of a comprehensive signal book that was refined through the late 1820s and finally agreed upon by 1831. Some of the more interesting signals which were defined give an insight into yachting at the time such as signals for: 'Can you lend me your band?' and 'Have you any Ladies onboard' to signals ashore such as 'one hundred prawns' and even one for 'three-hundred oysters'.

Lord Yarborough was appointed Commodore in 1825, although records suggest that he may well have been acknowledged as such by fellow members even earlier. Some reports suggest the date 1822, a time when he would have been the Member of Parliament for Lincolnshire which he served from 1807 to 1823.[2]

The presence of George Hamilton Chichester, the 3rd Marquess of Donegall, who held the courtesy title of the Viscount Chichester to 1799 before assuming the Earl of Belfast title, which he held from 1799 through to 1844, was something of a step change for The Royal Yacht Club and a perfect foil for the benign Lord Yarborough.

Appointed Vice Commodore in 1827, Lord Belfast swiftly arranged for a new club button to be designed (and then re-designed at his own expense in 1831), negotiated with the Admiralty for members to fly the distinctive White Ensign and then in 1833 was the diplomatic go-between with King William IV for the renaming of the club. In a letter dated 4 July 1833, Lord Belfast wrote to the secretary of the club:

> Sir, I have it in command from His Majesty to acquaint you for the information of the Commodore and the officers of the Royal Yacht Club that as a mark of His Majesty's gracious approval of an institution of such national utility, it is his gracious wish and pleasure that it shall

[2] Other appointments of this grand and generous man included being Master of the Brocklesby Hounds 1816–1846; the Recorder of Great Grimsby 1823–1832; the Recorder of Newport, Isle of Wight, 1825–1832; the Provincial Grand Master of Isle of Wight Freemasons 1826–1846; the Lt Colonel of the North Lincolnshire Regiment of Yeomanry 1831 and the Vice-Admiral of Hampshire and the Isle of Wight in 1831.

be henceforth known and styled the 'Royal Yacht Squadron' of which His Majesty is graciously pleased to consider himself the head.

The 'national utility' that His Majesty referred to was reference to the significant contribution that the Royal Yacht Squadron and its members made to the development of naval ships and the understanding that the Royal Navy regarded the club and its fleet as something of an auxiliary fleet. When Lord Belfast approached the famous shipbuilder Joseph White of Cowes in the early 1830s to build a 330-ton brigantine called *Waterwitch*, his racing intentions were unknown. Laid out in every way like a naval ten-gun brig, Lord Belfast trialled the yacht in a Royal Naval experimental squadron off Cork, Ireland, soon after her launch in 1832 and was so successful against the navy's fleet that the story back in Cowes was that she would be bought, and presumably copied henceforth, by His Majesty's service.

This didn't happen initially, but what is presumed to be the first ever offshore yacht race, in the autumn of 1834 between *Waterwitch* and the Welsh iron baron Christopher Rice Mansel Talbot's *Galatea*, brought much attention to Lord Belfast's creation. Over a 224-mile course out to the Eddystone Lighthouse, *Galatea* was actually bettering *Waterwitch* but on the way home lost her jib-boom and topmast allowing *Waterwitch* to overtake and win the private match. A week later the Admiralty purchased her.

Lord Yarborough and Lord Belfast steered the club through a time of growing interest in the sport of yachting and related nautical affairs. Their influence was far-reaching and their corralling of the membership around a common purpose was admirable. As Commodore and Vice Commodore, they also oversaw the transition of monarchy after King William IV's death at Windsor Castle with Queen Adelaide at his bedside and the subsequent accession of the 18-year-old Queen Victoria. Lord Conyngham, the Marquess of Anglesey's son-in-law, was present with the Archbishop of Canterbury to inform the new Queen of her uncle's death at 5 am on the 20 June 1837.

Lord Yarborough was more of a cruising man, often joining naval exercises, whilst Lord Belfast never owned a yacht again after selling *Waterwitch*. Lord Yarborough's yachting was severely hampered when in 1835, sailing onboard the club's flagship yacht, the 351-ton *Falcon*, he was thrown over a sea-chest in a gale which inflicted serious injury to his legs. This led to him downsizing the following year to a 156-ton cutter, the *Kestrel*, which he modified over time until in 1845, whilst cruising to Vigo in Spain, he suffered a heart attack and died unexpectedly at the age of 65.

The death of Lord Yarborough prompted a power struggle within the club hierarchy with Lord Belfast, the obvious candidate to assume the role of Commodore, gaining a boost to his candidacy when the Marquess of Anglesey, the assumed only other candidate that could stand, stated that he did not wish to be considered. Lord Belfast, by then the Marquess of Donegall, was instated at the May 1847 meeting of the club, but within the hierarchy moves were afoot to make his tenure short.

A resolution requiring the ownership of a yacht of a certain tonnage was promoted and denied and a further resolution questioning the Marquess of Donegall's qualifications was also denied whilst a cabal of members wrote to the *Morning Post* complaining about the Marquess lobbying for votes, something that was deemed most unseemly at the time. A political hotbed ensued at the club whilst the emergence of Thomas Egerton, the 2nd Earl of Wilton and someone who would become arguably the architect of the America's Cup and certainly one of the most influential people in the history of the competition, came to the fore.

Egerton was the second son of the 1st Marquess of Westminster, Robert Grosvenor, and his wife Lady Eleanor Egerton, daughter of Thomas Egerton, the 1st Earl of Wilton. In 1814, at the age of 14, Egerton succeeded to the earldom of Wilton according to a special remainder on the death of his maternal grandfather and also inherited Heaton Park in Manchester. On his 21st birthday, the now Lord Wilton, took his seat in the House of Lords and whilst his interests included music and horse racing (he established the Heaton Park Races in 1827), yachting and the Royal Yacht Squadron, where he came on to the list in 1832, were to dominate his life.

A serial yacht owner, between 1835 and 1853, Lord Wilton owned a string of large schooners that he named *Xarifa*, but what he couldn't have foreseen was the growing turmoil within the club that he so loved as the end of the 1840s approached. Issues over the flying of the White Ensign, the club's burgee, and the hub-bub around the Marquess of Donegall's appointment in 1847 as Commodore rumbled on. Eventually, and with his role untenable, the Marquess resigned his position in 1848 and by a unanimous vote in 1849, Lord Wilton took over the reins and set a course for history.

With the club politics so damaged, fleet numbers and subsequent racing either private or in regattas on the water suffered greatly. A practice had emerged in the mid-1840s of prospective members of the club buying yachts, becoming members, and then subsequently selling them whilst staying as active 'political' ponchos within the establishment. Elsewhere, regatta racing was surging with some 16 royal clubs dotted around the Solent and beyond, encouraging private wager racing as well as regattas for local boatmen with yachts of all sizes competing. The Cowes Regatta was dwindling so much that in 1849, the Queen's Cup, a cup once held in as great esteem as the King's Cup for member yachts in the 50–75-ton range, was so poorly attended by members that it had to be made an open race.

In the background to this decline, the Marquess of Anglesey remained a force within the club and was, in 1848, the instigator of a club race around the Isle of Wight. Races around the Isle of Wight had been recorded as far back as 1812, but for the new trophy, to be known as the 'RYS £100 Cup', the Marquess had happened upon a series of elaborate silver ewers that were crafted on spec by the Crown Jeweller R. & S. Garrard and were on display in a large showroom at 29–31 Panton Street, just off Leicester Square. R. & S. Garrard had been founded by George Wickes in 1735 in Mayfair, London, and it specialised in the elaborate manufacture of silver and jewellery, serving an ever wealthier upper and upper middle-class clientele.[3]

The ewers on display in the Garrard showroom were representative stock pieces and the Marquess purchased one for the sum of £100 with the explicit intention of donating it to the club. A large number of these ewers had been created to similar designs by master silversmith and chief designer at R. & S. Garrard, Edmund Cotterill. Incapable of holding liquids, they were in the wildly decorative presentation, neo-Mannerist silversmith-style of the mid-19th century known as eclecticism. Cotterill, who ran the Garrard design studio from 1833 onwards, employed a range of talented craftsmen,

[3] Robert Garrard joined the firm in 1792 and was succeeded by his three eldest sons Robert (Junior), James and Sebastian in 1818 who took over the management of the workshop and traded under the name 'R. J. and S. Garrard'. James Garrard, who eventually became Prime Warden of the Goldsmiths' Company in 1847, appears to have retired from the firm around 1835. From then until 1843, the year in which they succeeded Rundell, Bridge & Co. as the official Crown Jewellers in Queen Victoria's reign, Robert Garrard (Junior) and Sebastian Garrard continued trading under the style of R. & S. Garrard.

The company held the royal family patronage during six consecutive reigns, right up until 2007, receiving a number of important commissions and producing jewellery and silverware for the extended Royal Family. The company stayed in the hands of the Garrard family until 1952, when it merged with the Goldsmiths' and Silversmiths' Company of London.

sculptors, and artistic specialists. He was instrumental in building R. & S. Garrard into the foremost bespoke jeweller famed for producing elaborate sculptural groups and centrepieces in bronze and silver.

Cotterill had attended the Royal Academy Schools in 1820 and exhibited at the Academy from 1822 through to 1858 and at the British Institution from 1832 to 1855. *The Illustrated London News* stated that he was 'at the head of the class of artists who model for silversmiths and his productions, annually exhibited at Messrs Garrard, have earned that house a celebrity which no other can equal'. Such was his prestige that Prince Albert commissioned him in 1840 to make a model of his favoured greyhound Eos, which was later used again for a centrepiece produced in 1842. This piece was exhibited at the Annual Exhibition of British Manufacturers and is now displayed in the Victoria & Albert Museum.

The trophy that today is the America's Cup was by no means the most elaborate of the ewers that were on offer to the Marquess of Anglesey when he visited the showroom from his Old Burlington Street house in early 1848. Indeed, it is thought that he selected the least adorned; Cotterill's style was to incorporate lavish horse sculptures, inspired by Moorish and Arabian equestrian themes, onto base thematic cups of which the RYS £100 Cup was just that – plain by the standards of the day.

Standing at just 68.6 cm high with a circumference around its bulbous middle of some 91 cm, what is known today as the America's Cup is a curious, infuriating at times, mismatch of engraving fonts on its elaborate shields and adornments. Spelling mistakes, omissions and random, misplaced engravings characterise what to many is a stunning and almost revered trophy, its backstory fascinating as much as its future. Many go quiet in its presence and touching it is a no-no for all but a few. Examining it reveals history, and you can spend many hours just walking around, noting, and absorbing its message. The panels and scrolls are somewhat faded through time and polish – in particular the names of the finishers in the first race which require a magnifying glass to make out. But that's all part of the charm, and it remains, as it always will, a piece of Victorian magnificence that symbolises excellence.

An interesting comparison is The Queen's Cup, Ascot, which came up for auction at Christie's auction house in New York in 2010. This cup was first presented in 1861, but hallmarked 1848, and therefore created at the same time as what would become 'America's Cup'. It is a most elaborate affair but bears remarkable base identity to the ewer purchased by the Marquess of Anglesey. Christie's described it as being:

> Of ewer form, on circular foot chased with fruit, the baluster stem with three beaded scroll brackets, the lobed bowl chased with strapwork and applied with pendant fruit and flowers, the removable upper section formed as grassy hill set with a buffalo hunt, two Indians on horseback, the neck with foliate scrolls and strapwork, with double scroll handle, engraved *The Gift of Her Majesty the Queen, Ascot 1861*, with applied Royal Arms, *marked on bowl, grass, horses, buffalo and neck*, also stamped *R & S Garrard, PANTON ST LONDON*.

Another significant set of trophies, comparable to the cup purchased by the Marquess, but again far more elaborate, was created for the Eglinton Tournament of 1839. What was created originally to mark that date, and now sits at Cunninghame House in Ayrshire, was a forerunner to the ewer style. It was an important marker in silver working with the components being manufactured separately and then assembled for the final design, as was the case with The America's Cup. The original trophy was intended as a centrepiece of gothic mediaeval design with shields bearing the coats of arms of the 14 'Knights of the Tournament'. A 15th shield is blank and four of the shields are placed in alcoves that extend from the base, accompanied by swords, quills, coronets and laurel leaf crown. The 140 cm-high trophy rises up as a highly ornate gothic pulpit sitting beneath a pinnacled canopy under which Jane Georgiana, Lady Seymour, the Queen of Beauty, stands in the act of placing a wreath upon the brow of the Earl of Eglinton, Lord and victor of the Eglinton Tournament.

Whilst that trophy survives, a second Eglinton trophy, believed to have been crafted at the same time as the America's Cup in 1848, was presented to Archibald, Earl of Eglinton by some 300 citizens of Glasgow to celebrate the famous re-enactment of a mediaeval joust on his Ayrshire estate. Very little survives of this trophy other than a small statuette of a knight in full armour with a jousting lance and a horse bearing the Earl of Eglinton's coat of arms. Elaborate line drawings commissioned at the time serve as reference today as the candelabrum, very similar to the base of the America's Cup, was melted down for its silver after being sold by the Earl of Eglinton in the 1920s to settle a tax bill on his land.

Cotterill's display at the Great Exhibition of 1851 was regarded as unmissable for visitors.[4] His legacy of craftsmanship, quite apart from The America's Cup, includes trophies that are still competed for today at Ascot, Doncaster and Goodwood. With the Cup secured, it is now the longest continually contested international sports trophy in the world. The Marquess of Anglesey's delivery of the Cup arguably saved both the club, to which he was a founding member (albeit in absentia), and, indeed, racing on the south coast, whilst cementing its place in the annals of international sailing forevermore.

[4] The Tsar of Russia purchased one of the 1848 series of ewers, described in *The Illustrated London News* thus:

> On its base are seen the figure of Hercules, who, having destroyed the tyrant Diomedes, is about to strike with his club one of the horses. The figure of the god is admirably delineated; it is a perfect model of strength, activity, bodily and mental energy. The vase itself rises from the base ... and is appropriately decorated with figurative emblems of the Labours of Hercules. In the front is one of the birds of Stymphalus, an Arcadian lake. The handle of the Vase is formed of the folds of the Hydra. The ornaments are all in allusion to the labours of the principal figure. There are the heads of the boar, the stag, the bull, and the dog Cerberus, properly introduced and aiding in the general design.

The sparsely populated area of the United States room at the Great Exhibition in 1851.

CHAPTER TWO

THE GREAT EXHIBITION OF THE WORKS OF INDUSTRY OF ALL NATIONS – 1851

The surmounting of problems that most sensible people considered insurmountable.[1]

Very much the vision of Prince Albert, the Great Exhibition of the Works of Industry of all Nations played a highly significant, yet almost unseen, hand in the creation of what would become the America's Cup. Despite not being built specifically for the Great Exhibition, the yacht *America* was to do much to salvage American pride at a difficult time in its history. Queen Victoria's involvement and visible acknowledgement of the yacht and its gentlemen who behaved so impeccably in victory was to start something of great significance between the two countries.

An estimated 400,000 well-wishers lined the streets of London from Buckingham Palace to Westminster Abbey for the Coronation of Queen Victoria on 28 June 1838. The previous year, her uncle William IV had died early in the morning, and she had immediately assumed the throne. Victoria's father, Prince Edward, the Duke of Kent and Strathearn, had been the fourth son of George III and Queen Charlotte and had died in 1820, the year after her birth.

Before the birth of Victoria, George III's only legitimate grandchild had been Princess Charlotte of Wales, the only child of his eldest son, the Prince Regent, who was to succeed him as George IV. Princess Charlotte's death in 1817, the result of childbirth to a stillborn son, precipitated a crisis of succession, which brought pressure on the unmarried younger brothers of

[1] From Queen Victoria's Journal (1851).

the Prince Regent, including William, Duke of Clarence, and Edward, Duke of Kent, to marry and have legitimate offspring. In 1818, the Duke of Clarence married Princess Adelaide of Saxe-Meiningen, while the Duke of Kent proposed to and married Marie Louise Victoire, the Dowager Duchess of Leiningen, a widowed German princess who already had two children by her first marriage to Emich Carl, the 2nd Prince of Leiningen. The Clarences remained childless, while the Duke and Duchess of Kent's only child, Victoria, was born at 4.15 am on 24 May 1819 in the dining room at Kensington Palace in London – the closest room for the maids to fetch warm water from the kitchens.

Victoria's childhood, which she recalled sometime later in adulthood as being 'lonely and unhappy', was set within a protective bubble designed by her mother, the then widowed Duchess of Kent, and instigated by her ambitious comptroller Sir John Conroy, equerry to the late Duke, who had eyes on creating significant control within the royal household should Victoria inherit the throne before the age of 18. This eventuality would have made the Duchess 'Regent'. Victoria's only ally was her 'beloved governess Baroness Lehzen', according to the Historic Royal Palace's account. William IV, who ascended to the throne in 1820, was so mistrusting of the Duchess's abilities, and the role played by Conroy, that he declared most publicly, in front of her in 1836, that he wished to live to see Victoria turn 18 in order to avoid a regency.

Victoria, confined to Kensington Palace playing with her dolls, took an interest in art and doodling, whilst her King Charles Spaniel 'Dash' was a welcome distraction. The regime, which became known as the 'Kensington System', or just the 'System', stipulated rules and protocols in order to avoid Victoria mixing with 'undesirables'. It had been developed by the Duchess and Conroy, rumoured by their detractors to be lovers, in order to make the future Queen dependent upon them.

Victoria slept in her mother's chambers and was privately tutored with a concentration on the arts and singing (she even had lessons from the opera singer Luigi Lablache), alongside regular day-trips around England. Victoria disliked this exposure to the public almost as much as her uncle William IV had done. Writing in her journal, she noted, 'The country is very desolate … everywhere smoking and burning coal heaps, intermingled with wretched huts and carts and little ragged children.' In May 1836, on her 17th birthday, Victoria was introduced by her favourite uncle, and father-figure, King Leopold I of Belgium, to her cousin, the man who would become the love of her life and a true force in Victorian Britain, Prince Albert of Saxe-Coburg and Gotha.

A year later on the 20 June 1837, just one month after her 18th birthday and coming of age, King William IV died at Windsor Castle at the age of 71. She recalled the morning in her journal: 'I got out of bed and went into my sitting-room (only in my dressing-gown), and alone, and saw them. Lord Conyngham (the Lord Chamberlain) then acquainted me that my poor Uncle, the King, was no more, and had expired at 12 minutes past two this morning, and consequently that I am Queen.' In the months before his passing, Victoria had been presented as 'The Nation's hope' and the Victorian era of Great Britain, in which the early story of the America's Cup is set, began on a positive note. Her reign, that would last until her death in 1901, had begun.

She was a queen, not yet in wedlock, with a mother that she had banished to remote apartments in Buckingham Palace. Although it was with much affection that the young queen was initially received by the British public and journals of the day, only marriage could break the cycle of the Duchess and Conroy. With growing affection for Prince Albert, it was Victoria who proposed to him on the 15 October 1839.

They were married in February 1840 at the Chapel Royal of St James's Palace and in her diaries, she wrote:

> I never, never spent such an evening! My dearest, dearest, dear Albert ... his excessive love & affection gave me feelings of heavenly love & happiness I never could have hoped to have felt before! He clasped me in his arms, & we kissed each other again & again! His beauty, his sweetness & gentleness – really how can I ever be thankful enough to have such a Husband! ... to be called by names of tenderness, I have never yet heard used to me before – was bliss beyond belief! Oh! This was the happiest day of my life.

The Britain that Queen Victoria and Prince Albert presided over was a country slowly on the up, about to undergo remarkable industrial, political, scientific and military change, alongside a vast expansion of the British Empire. Throughout her reign, Queen Victoria enjoyed wide popularity within the Empire and even into the New World where her influence was extraordinary. Her wedding was viewed with intense fascination by the American public and, as we will see later in the story of the *America* – the yacht that won the first race around the Isle of Wight in 1851, Victoria's astute antenna for the coming of the New World changed the course of public discussion and profile.

The *United States Magazine and Democratic Review*, an influential political and literary magazine, disparagingly termed her influence in the United States as 'Victoria Fever', an anti-republican 'Queen-mania' that started before the coronation and continued after. The *Smithsonian* magazine even quoted an anonymous writer who said that in Philadelphia souvenir hairbrushes could be found with Victoria's picture on them, 'Victoria soap, composed expressly for the coronation' and 'Victoria riding hats', among other things. The writer even suggested that by the time he left Philadelphia he had seen so much evidence of the new Queen's influence that he suggested changing the city's name to 'Victoria-delphia'. But it was a national interest, spreading wide across the country, and her coronation was viewed with endless fascination. Lengthy column inches were granted to cover everything from the minutiae of the pageantry, the size and provenance of the jewels in her crown, to the white dress she wore, which inspired and reinvigorated the tradition for white weddings amongst the Victorian elites that lasts to this day and is ubiquitously accepted.

At her side, as she grappled with the first years of ascension to the throne, was Prince Albert, one of the most complex of personalities. With his restless nature, he threw himself into the epicentre of politics, regarding it almost as the first call on his time, whilst running the vast estates of Balmoral (which he renovated and added to), Windsor and Buckingham Palace, plus overseeing the building and extensive groundworks and gardens of Osborne House on the Isle of Wight. His energies knew no bounds, but it was many a physician that called for him to rest, such was his closeness to exhaustion, or what Queen Victoria would later describe as being 'fagged out'.

One of the biggest influences on Prince Albert's life was his working relationship with Henry Cole, the Keeper of the Public Records, who by all accounts was a most remarkable individual. Cole shared the prince's love of arts, architecture, music and design, in particular industrial design. He had pioneered the introduction of the Penny Post, had campaigned successfully for the standard gauge railway track to be adopted and was a children's author. Henry Cole also ran the South Kensington Museum for over 20 years and would eventually go on to be in charge of both the Royal College of Music and the Royal Albert Hall in London.

A whirlwind of ambition, spirit and imagination, Henry Cole connected with Prince Albert on many levels. In 1846, Cole joined the Society of Arts and together the two put on shows, displays and exhibitions that concentrated on manufacturing design, the first of which was in 1847, the year that the Society had received its Royal Charter. By 1849, visitor numbers to the exhibitions had sky-rocketed to over 100,000 and the first thoughts of a National Quintennial Exhibition were mooted.

Scholars debate whether it was actually Cole's suggestion but the accepted wisdom, and indeed credit, has always fallen to Prince Albert. What is of record in the National Archives in Kew, London, are the original letters of Cole who laid out a vision and a desire to hold an exhibition based on the French Exposition format that he had visited in 1849 in Paris. Also in those papers is the record of Prince Albert and Cole in discussion insisting that any grand exhibitions 'must embrace foreign productions' and promote 'international certainty'.

'The Great Exhibition of the Works of Industry of all Nations' was thus conceived, and a date was set for opening on the 1 May 1851. Henry Cole was sent on a national tour, along with Scott Russell, the Society's Secretary, replete with a letter of authorisation from Prince Albert, charging them 'to travel throughout the manufacturing districts of the country, in order to collect the opinions of the leading manufacturers concerning a Great Exhibition to be held in London in the year 1851.' Upon Cole's and Russell's return, some '5000 influential persons' had agreed to act as promoters.

Suddenly the idea started to develop momentum. Prince Albert used his position to secure a Royal Commission in 1850, with less than a year to opening, to take over the project, such was the importance of its success to the nation. A venue had to be secured, but the prince's original idea of taking over Leicester Square was rejected in favour of Hyde Park. This caused consternation among a very vocal chattering and political class in London at the time, described by one Windsor Castle adviser as 'Orators who object to everything and would sacrifice an undertaking to the pleasure of making a smart speech'.

Indeed, it was to the satirical but highly influential magazine of *Punch* that a most stinging rebuke came for the proposal to hold the Great Exhibition in Hyde Park:

Albert! Spare those trees,
Mind where you fix your show.
For Mercy's sake, don't please,
Go spoiling Rotten Row.

With consent required by the House of Commons for the show to proceed, the entire project was almost derailed by the publication in *The Illustrated London News*, on 22 June 1850, of a permanent structure that would require some 19 million bricks to build. It was panned in the media, Prince Albert detested the design, but by some margin the overall project was passed by the politicians in a well-whipped vote of the Lower House.

By chance, in London at the House of Commons that day, was Joseph Paxton, onsite to revamp the acoustics of the new chamber. Paxton was much admired as an architect by Queen Victoria and Prince Albert after they had visited the Great Conservatory at Chatsworth in 1843. Completed in 1840, the Great Conservatory was, at the time, the largest glass building in England at 84 metres long, 37 metres wide and 19 metres high. Inside there was room for two carriages to pass on the main thoroughfare, and stairs, hidden by ascending rocks, led to a gallery from which visitors could inspect the highest branches of the exotic palms and other trees flourishing there. There were ponds full of aquatic plants, rocks, mosses, ferns and brilliantly coloured flowers in a tropical climate.

Feeling the temperature of the House of Commons that day, Paxton realised that a great mistake was about to unfold in the design of the Great Exhibition. Armed with woolly sketches, he set about in just nine days working with his team to create a masterplan which he then presented to a flustered Executive Committee. He published his designs in *The Illustrated London News* on the 6 June 1850, and it was again the satirical magazine *Punch* that picked up on the proposals and nicknamed it 'The Crystal Palace'. Prince Albert was so impressed that he called it 'the most advanced and wonderful building of the 19th century.' On 15 July 1850, Paxton's design was unanimously accepted on the condition that three enormous elm trees be housed within its structure. The foundations began to be laid by August that year.

The structure rose rapidly, becoming a wonder of the time, a triumph of the Victorian age, and by March 1851 it was complete. Inside the vast halls, the Exhibition was divided into six main areas encompassing raw materials, machinery, textiles, metallic, vitreous and ceramic manufactures, miscellaneous and Fine Arts, with some 30 classes within these main categories. In total, some 100,000 exhibits were on display, with the centrepiece undoubtedly housed within the magnificent Indian section, the Koh-i-Noor diamond standing in a 1.9 metre-high cage, provided by Charles & Jeremiah Chubb, which was locked to the floor. Weighing some 186.5

carats at the time, the diamond, although the centrepiece and a marvel of the age, was so lacking brilliance that Prince Albert had it re-cut after the exhibition by Sebastian Garrard and reduced it to 105 carats. Queen Victoria was always said to be 'embarrassed' in owning the diamond owing to its provenance of being looted from Lahore, India, by British Forces.

Other wonderments and curiosities at the Great Exhibition included a fire engine made of galvanised iron, a portable cleansing machine, the patented water closet and steam engines of every description. There was an oscillating cylinder that particularly attracted Prince Albert's eye, an 80-blade penknife, a papier-mâché piano, Milanese statues by Puttinati, tapestries by Gobelins and James Nasmyth's ingenious steam-hammer. A giant rubber boat made by the entrepreneur Charles Goodyear was yet another of the extraordinaries on display for the Victorian public. The visitors who flocked there were numbered in millions – with some estimates putting that figure as high as six million during the course of the Exhibition, which ran from 1 May through to 11 October 1851.

The sheer scale of the Great Exhibition was astonishing with a length over three times that of St Paul's Cathedral and a total of 293,655 panes of bespoke glass. Holding it together was a masterclass of construction and engineering with some 4,500 tons of iron and no less than 24 miles of guttering – a vital consideration in London, even in summer.

Prince Albert's dedication, mirrored by master architect and the rightfully-to-be knighted Paxton, to every last, minute detail undoubtedly produced a remarkable result: at the age of just 32 he had created and curated one of the truly great exhibitions of the world. In a letter to his grandmother, just before the opening, he wrote of the toll it took on his health saying: 'Just at present, I am more dead than alive from overwork'. As the opening day neared, Prince Albert's problems only grew with a political firestorm erupting stirred by the then Foreign Secretary, Lord Palmerston, around the *Corps Diplomatique* presentation at the opening ceremony, with Palmerston attesting in writing that the Corps should be invited to attend the opening as 'spectators and not as actors' which went down badly with both the Queen and the Prince.

Further problems arose from the Austrians, Prussians, French and Russians around security issues and the hysterical notion of assassination attempts. There were problems too with the British and Foreign Bible Society and even a ruckus, which amused the Queen, when a wigmaker who had wished to be positioned in the Fine Arts section found himself in the 'Animal Products' section. Perhaps the icing on the cake was the insistence that the gun salute be moved from Hyde Park to St. James's Park on the grounds that the reverberations of the cannon shot could cause the windows of the Crystal Palace to shatter.

Rising above the endless commotion, Prince Albert played a trump card that none of the gentry or the media saw coming. The Queen herself would open the Exhibition on the 1 May 1851. Security was naturally an issue, so little did the Royal family mingle with their public, but Albert's insistence on making the monarchy and indeed the whole family more accessible and more visible was a theme that the Queen entertained. Hurried negotiations took place at senior government department level, including with Lord John Russell, 1st Earl of Russell, the Prime Minister of the day, and after deliberations it was decided to allow 'season ticket' holders to attend the opening.

A balcony salute from Buckingham Palace, the 'Albert balcony', on the morning of the opening of the Crystal Palace preceded the Royal party making their way the short distance to Hyde Park by carriage as tens of thousands lined the route. Queen Victoria would record the occasion in her personal journal on Thursday 1 May 1851:

> This day is one of the greatest and most glorious days of our lives, with which, to my pride and joy the name of my dearly beloved Albert is for ever associated! It is a day which makes my heart swell with thankfulness ... The Park presented a wonderful spectacle, crowds streaming through it, carriages and troops passing, quite like the Coronation Day, and for me, the same anxiety.
>
> The day was bright, and all bustle and excitement. At half past 11, the whole procession, in nine state carriages, was set in motion ... Bertie was in full Highland dress. The Green Park and Hyde Park were one mass of densely crowded human beings, in the highest good humour and most enthusiastic. I never saw Hyde Park look as it did, being filled with crowds as far as the eye could reach. A little rain fell, just as we started, but before we neared the Crystal Palace, the sun shone and gleamed upon the gigantic edifice, upon which the flags of every nation were flying. We drove up Rotten Roe [sic] and got out of our carriages at the entrance in that side. The glimpse through the iron gates of the Transept, the waving palms and flowers, the myriads of people filling the galleries and seats around, together with the flourish of trumpets,

as we entered the building, gave a sensation I shall never forget, and I felt much moved. We went for a moment into a little room where we left our cloaks and found Mama and Mary. Outside all the Princes were standing. In a few seconds we proceeded, Albert leading me; having Vicky at his hand, and Bertie holding mine. The sight as we came to the centre where the steps and chair (on which I did not sit) was placed, facing the beautiful crystal fountain was magic and impressive. The tremendous cheering, the joy expressed in every face, the vastness of the building, with all its decorations and exhibits, the sound of the organ (with 200 instruments and 600 voices, which seemed nothing), and my beloved Husband the creator of this great 'Peace Festival', inviting the industry and art of all nations of the earth, all this, was indeed moving, and a day to live forever. God bless my dearest Albert, and my dear Country which has shown itself so great today. One felt so grateful to the great God, whose blessing seemed to pervade the whole great undertaking.

After the National Anthem had been sung, Albert left my side, and at the head of the Commissioners, – a curious assemblage of political and distinguished men, – read the Report to me, which is a long one, and I read a short answer. After this the Archbishop of Canterbury offered up a short and appropriate Prayer, followed by the singing of Handel's Hallelujah Chorus, during which time the Chinese Mandarin came forward and made his obeisance. This concluded, the Procession of great length began which was beautifully arranged, the prescribed order, being exactly adhered to. The Nave was full of people, which had not been intended and deafening cheers and waving of handkerchiefs, continued the whole time of our long walk from one end of the building, to the other. Every face was bright and smiling, and many even, had tears in their eyes. Many Frenchmen called out 'Vive la Reine'.

One could of course see nothing, but what was high up in the Nave, and nothing in the Courts. The organs were but little heard, but the Military Band, at one end, had a very fine effect, playing the March from 'Athalie', as we passed along. The old Duke of Wellington and Lord Anglesey walked arm in arm, which was a touching sight. I saw many acquaintances, amongst those present. We returned to our place and Albert told Lord Breadalbane to declare the Exhibition to be opened, which he did in a loud voice saying: 'Her Majesty Commands me to

> declare the Exhibition opened', when there was a flourish of trumpets, followed by immense cheering. We then made our bow and left.
>
> All those Commissioners, the Executive Committee, who had worked so hard and to whom such immense praise is due, seemed truly happy, and no one more so than Paxton, who may feel justly proud. He rose from an ordinary gardener's boy!
>
> Everyone was astounded & delighted. The return was equally satisfactory, – the crowd most enthusiastic and perfect order kept ... That we felt happy and thankful, – I need not say, – proud of all that had passed and of my beloved one's success. I was more impressed by the scene I had witnessed than words can say. Dearest Albert's name is for ever immortalised and the absurd reports of dangers of every kind & sort, set about by a set of people, – the 'soidisant' fashionables & the most violent protectionists, – are silenced. It is therefore doubly satisfactory that all should have gone off so well, and without the slightest accident or mishap. Phipps and Col. Seymour spoke to me with such pride and joy, at my beloved one's success & vindication, after so much opposition and such difficulties, which no one, but he with his good temper, patience, firmness and energy could have achieved. Without these qualities his high position alone, could not have carried him through.

With the broadsheet and journal media onside, the Exhibition silenced the naysayers, and with some 60,000 people a day attending initially, London and more specifically Hyde Park was the centre of the world. The Crystal Palace was adorned with every flag of the world and marked a point in time of mechanisation, displaying the now and the future. The times were moving forward with gusto and, although gaudy in places, elaborate beyond belief in others, the Victorians were on the cusp of a new age with Britain proudly at the centre with an almost 'whatever you can do, we can do better' mentality. The underlying theme was that Britain was the epicentre of manufacturing and innovation, so whilst other countries may have unique glitz or localised expertise, nobody could compete with Britain under the reign of Queen Victoria. Her Majesty herself was portrayed in a colossal sculpture cast in zinc – oh so mid-19th century!

America, however, was not so well received. A country barely a century old, the stuffiness and aloof nature of the gentry in Britain harboured perceived and ingrained hostility towards the New World. On a daily basis, every opportunity was taken by the newspapers and respected journals (and indeed the satirical magazines were some of the worst) in doing down America. Derogatory terms such as 'The Yankee' or 'Cousin' appeared in script whilst crude cartoons of Red Indians and in-your-face cartoons depicting slavery, that are still shocking today, appeared in the magazines at every opportunity. Queen Victoria herself appeared to stoke the flames in her journal when admiring the display of Sheffield Steel knives, including vicious-looking bowie knives, at the Exhibition remarked that they were: 'made for Americans who never move without one.' The notion of savagery was made most assertively but arguably, as we will see later in this book, this remark was perhaps out of character and an aberration for a forward-looking Queen pushed on by her devoted and much-loved Albert.

During America's first 100 years of existence, the search for a characterisation, which the nation could see as representative, took on many forms. There was Columbia, a rather feminine figure, the indigenous bald eagle, the stoic Lady Liberty and the buffoonery of 'Yankee Doodle'. The latter was originally a British invention – a caricature of a naive, upstart American colonist created as a foil for 'John Bull', the thunderously imposing personification of all that was perceived as good and stoic in Great Britain. After the Revolutionary War, 'Yankee Doodle' was developed into 'Brother Jonathan', a rustic New Englander characterised as a peddler, a seaman and a trader, and always as a sly, cunning and untrustworthy figure. It was a term that the British media and journals latched onto, alternating with 'Yankee' and 'Yankee Doodle' in derogatory terms.

Further perceptions of America, which trickled down and seeped into the public conscience, revolved around slavery and the slave trade. Whilst following a financial crisis in 1841 and 1842 when several states reneged on their debts and British investors lost all their money, Americans were meanly cast as dishonest. To add further indignity, the pirating of British boats and the clamour around the practice with the aid of the steamship routes, further built the negative narrative stirred up by Fleet Street and enhanced by the popular journals that had such mass appeal and directed public opinion.

The final throwaway remark often used by the aristocracy was around American's perceived brashness and crudity – very much not the Victorian gentleman's way. Whilst the rise of Republicanism did not so much threaten British societal structure, the population of the US, by 1851, stood at two thirds of Britain's census of 21,121,967 citizens, which was deemed alarming in academic quarters in Britain.

For the Great Exhibition itself, the American government did not officially involve itself and left the exhibits and overall organisation to the National Institute of America to provide, led by a distinguished and rather excitable committee. The structure of the Exhibition ensured that British manufacturers held 50 per cent of the not inconsiderable floor space, and that the rest of the nations would be allocated space according to their own estimates forwarded in advance to the working committee of the Exhibition. The American organisers made a grave miscalculation at the outset, perhaps in anticipation but almost certainly in exuberance, applying for the second largest overseas allocation beside France.

With goods laden from America, the steamship *St. Lawrence* arrived at Southampton Docks in the middle of March 1851 and was unloaded with a variety of New World inventions and advances. Particular attention was drawn to the array of Colt branded revolver pistols, various examples of advanced locksmithery, a cotton-engine (or 'cotton-gin'), Charles Goodyear's array of Indian rubber (including the boat), the first commercially available silver copper plate photographic processing devices (the daguerreotypes named after the French inventor Louis Jacques Mandé Daguerre), a Lerow & Blodgett sewing machine (the American Isaac Singer's patented invention of 1851 did not appear), transparent soaps, Cincinnati pickles, Virginia honey, dental appliances, a patented double grand piano, an air-exhausted coffin and even a model of a floating church design. American sculptors, notably Hiram Power and Peter Stephenson, sent works depicting a Greek Slave and a dying Indian respectively and there were minor curiosities such as a gossamer wig and a buck-eyed squirrel – all 'quaint' in their way but the source of derision and ridicule by the British media.

Indeed, such was the rampant vitriol espoused by the native journalists that some even remarked, after seeing the American exhibits sparsely laid out in the enormous space that had been commissioned, that the organisers should sub-let the space and allow migrants to be housed. The fact was that the organisers ended up putting benching within the Americana space to allow visitors to sit and rest their weary legs – a fact that some journalists opined was the only reason for any footfall at all within the section. The American juror who sat on the awards committee for the Exhibition (every country was represented), Horace Greener, wrote that: 'the hit in this case is certainly a fair one', and although objects such as the Colt pistols gained rave reviews, the overall effect of the Exhibition was to do nothing to enhance America's reputation in the Old World.

The Illustrated London News showcased the short-fallings of American bureaucrats on the 17 May 1851: 'There are very few of their manufacturers which could hope to sell here. American manufacturers of the same kind as those exported from Europe could only be sent as a matter of curiosity by a Government organisation. Private individuals seldom take such useless trouble.'

Punch (XX, 1851) put it even more strongly, saying at the same time,

> The Americans say, that the reason they have sent nothing to the exhibition is that the productions of their industry are too gigantic to be brought over and the reality is so impossible to be understood or described, that the only way to give us any idea of it was to leave it all to our imagination.

The journal doubled down further saying: 'Why not have sent us some choice specimens of slaves? We have the Greek Captive in dead stone, why not the Virginian slave in living ebony?' Before going on to list a number of 'American Contributions' which were alleged to be on their way including: 'the tremendous wooden style that separates the American from the English fields of literature.'

In setting out his vision for the Great Exhibition, Prince Albert made a speech at the Mansion House in 1849 with a novel world vision that was years ahead of his time. In it he stated most clearly:

> Nobody who has paid any attention to the peculiar features of our present era, will doubt for a moment that we are living at a period of most wonderful transition, which tends rapidly to accomplish that great end, to which, indeed, all history points – the realisation of the unity of mankind. Not a unity which breaks down the limits and levels the peculiar characteristics of the different nations of the earth, but rather a unity, the result and product of those very national varieties and antagonistic qualities. The distances which separated the different nations and parts of the globe are rapidly vanishing before the achievements of modern invention, and we can traverse them with incredible ease; the languages of all nations are known, and their acquirement placed within the reach of everybody; thought is communicated with the rapidity, and even by the power, of lightning. On the other hand, the great principle of division of labour, which may be called the moving power of civilisation, is being extended to all branches of science, industry, and art. Whilst formerly the greatest mental energies strove at universal knowledge, and that knowledge was

confined to the few, now they are directed on specialities, and in these, again, even to the minutest points; but the knowledge acquired becomes at once the property of the community at large; for, whilst formerly discovery was wrapped in secrecy, the publicity of the present day causes that no sooner is a discovery or invention made than it is already improved upon and surpassed by competing efforts. The products of all quarters of the globe are placed at our disposal, and we have only to choose which is the best and the cheapest for our purposes, and the powers of production are entrusted to the stimulus of competition and capital.

Where the committee of the National Institute of America failed in the public's eye, what was brewing in the yachting world was to be revelatory and amply echoed the sentiments of 'unity' that Prince Albert so eloquently described in his speech. Unbeknown and certainly unacknowledged at first by the shambolic and political National Institute, a small group from the then six-year-old New York Yacht Club, was putting together a bold campaign to show American shipbuilding in its finest light, stun the established British fleets and rock the yachting establishment to its very core. The campaign's success, however, was to have far-reaching socio-political consequences and all of them universally positive.

In the very last barbed attack on the New World of 1851, *Punch* took aim at the coming of the yacht *America* to British shores with a satirical and back-handed swipe:

> We are informed the *America* yacht is about to be purchased by a distinguished book selling firm in New York for the purpose of running between that city and London. This is characteristically wise of publishing Jonathan. If you will live by robbing the brains of others it is only the more prudent to outstrip all competitors in the earliest possession of the stolen goods.

The historian and academic Marcus Cunliffe, writing in the *American Quarterly*, a 100 years after the Great Exhibition, reviewed the American contribution:

> In fact both Britain and America could feel well pleased by the results of the Great Exhibition. The latter had recovered from a bad start, the former had accomplished what it set out to do in acting as both host and hero in a superbly staged entertainment. The sense of her own primacy undoubtedly encouraged the journalists of Britain to temper their

> observations on the United States. At the same time, it had to be admitted that America had compelled respect and like all good entertainments this one concealed a number of moral lessons. One was that emotion played quite as greater part as rational thought in determining Anglo American relations. Heat seemed easier to generate than light.

What would occur in the summer of 1851 with the arrival of the *America* and the subsequent impeccable grace with which the syndicate owners (only three of them travelled with the yacht – Commodore Stevens, his brother Edwin Stevens and Colonel A. Hamilton) conducted themselves was to do much to repair reputations and build new bridges between the Old and New Worlds.

The Lawson History of the America's Cup (1902), which covered the first 50 years of the competition in detail, and is widely seen as the authority on the early years, states:

> Prior to their appearance in England with the America there had been very little social intercourse between the two countries whose relations were by no means as close as they are now. The managers of the America were pioneers in international sporting events, which naturally have an important social side. Their experiences in England did more good than could be appreciated at the time.

Queen Victoria was not immune to public and media sentiment. Although only into her second decade on the throne, and still in her 30s, her innate sense for how the Empire and the world were advancing with change all around, amplified by the success and innovation on the display at the Great Exhibition that year, culminated in a most extraordinary way and did much to stem the tide of negativity around the United States. Arguably the forerunner for what would become known as the 'special relationship', much later in history between the United State and Great Britain, Queen Victoria's actions that summer of 1851 and thereafter did much to seal the bond between the two countries. The yacht *America* and its gentlemen owners were arguably the catalysts.

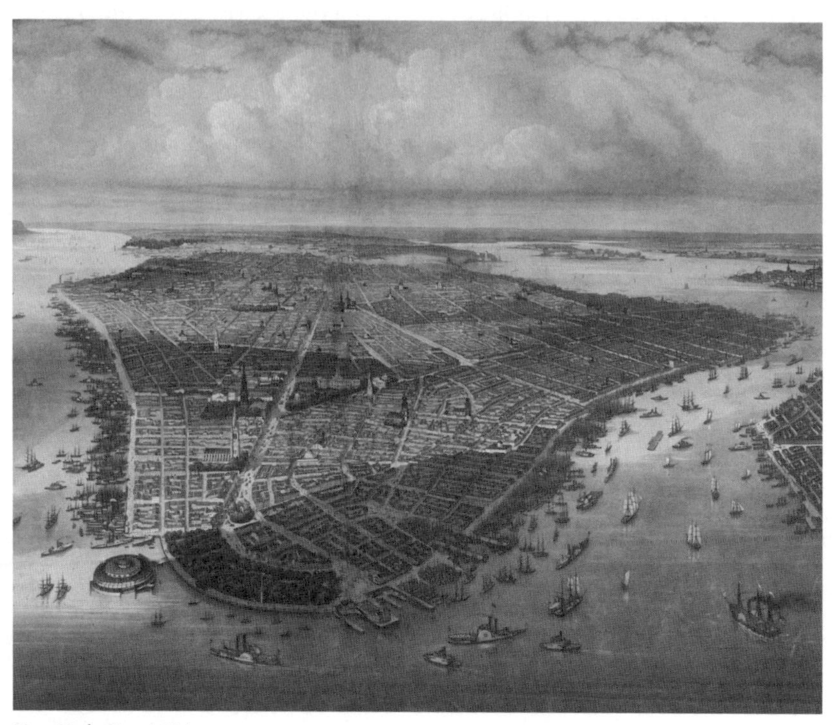

New York City, 1851.

CHAPTER THREE

JOHN COX STEVENS AND THE NEW YORK YACHT CLUB

They have a club-house – a handsome Gothic cottage – erected for the use of the club in a pleasant grove in the Elysian Fields, by that prince of good fellows, John C. Stevens who makes the punch, superintends the cooking, and presides at the table, under the appropriate title of Commodore.[1]

Whilst both the Marquess of Anglesey and the Earl of Wilton must rightly take enormous credit for the events that led up to the most famous race in sailing history, without the influence of a certain John Cox Stevens, the contest would never have happened. A most remarkable individual by all accounts, greatly admired by his peers and with sailing coursing through his veins from an early age, Stevens propelled American seamanship and boatbuilding onto a global stage with considerable grace, earning him praise in the highest circles of society, and he is revered even to this day.

Born on 24 September 1785 to Colonel John Stevens III and mother Rachel Cox he grew up surrounded by boats, with his father not only being a lawyer and engineer by trade but a pioneer in the soon-to-be-burgeoning industry of steamboats. In 1802, Col. Stevens built a screw-driven steamboat and, buoyed by its success, went on to build one of the first ocean-going steamboats, the *Phoenix*, which sailed to the Delaware River in 1809. The father of 13 children, Col. Stevens had served in George Washington's army and was later appointed as the Treasurer of New Jersey between 1776 and 1779, after which time he happened to purchase at auction in 1784 a

[1] From *The Diary of Philip Hone* (1846). Philip Hone was Mayor of New York City from 1826 to 1827. He was notable for the detailed diary that he kept from 1828 until the time of his death in 1851. This diary is said to be the most extensive and detailed in existence in the first half of 19th-century America.

mosquito-infested, largely discarded, swamp-land which had been confiscated from a Tory landowner.

This land, which was known then as 'William Bayard's farm at Hoebuck', is now the bustling city of Hoboken, but at the time it became home to the very first site and proving-ground of American railroads. John Stevens is still known today as the 'Father of the US Railroad'. That title was proven after Stevens built a circular railroad track on William Bayard's farmstead and demonstrated the feasibility of steam locomotion, mirroring the pioneering work going on in Britain by the inventor George Stephenson. Incidentally, Stephenson's son, Robert, was a keen yachtsman, later owning the schooner *Titania*, and it was he who was granted the first railroad charter in North America in 1815.

Meanwhile the pioneering Stevens also ran the world's first commercial steam ferry company from 1811, initially plying the profitable New Jersey and Hoboken to New York, Hudson River routes albeit amidst stern competition from Robert Fulton's eponymous ferry company. The night ferry up to Albany, a most luxurious affair for the very wealthiest of New York citizens to reach the Berkshires, Saratoga and the great camps of the Adirondacks, became the *à la mode* way to avoid dusty rail carriages for those with means and the Stevens brothers profited.

Having had a happy childhood spent at the water's edge, John Cox Stevens, the eldest of the 13 children, had a passion for yachts and was very much seen as the sporting son of the family, eager to promote boating most keenly with his closest brother Edwin Augustus Stevens, who would later himself become Commodore of the New York Yacht Club.

Before graduating from Columbia University, formerly 'Kings College' as a result of royal charter by King George II of Great Britain, at the age of just 18, the young Stevens had built his first boat named *Diver*, in 1802, which he raced off the family's Hoboken dock against the various yachts that plied up and down the Hudson River. Racing was in his blood, and he would often bet with his brothers on the outcome. It certainly wasn't to be his last boat and his fascination with the extreme tidal waters off New Jersey and his father's foreshore at Hoboken inspired a lifetime's passion.

After graduation he naturally fell into the family business, and when the opportunity was afforded by his father in 1811, he took over the running of steam ferry operations that would ultimately become highly profitable. As success followed, he built *Trouble* in 1814 and then a catamaran that he named *Double Trouble* in 1820, before his first schooner *Wave* in 1832.

Aside from yachting, Stevens was passionate about horses and with that world came the inevitable fascination with betting. He was President of the Jockey Club at one point in the early 1820s and through this went on to set up the controversial and well-documented Great North–South Match of 27 May 1823, an endurance race between the horses 'The Eclipse' (from the north) and the 'Sir Henry' (from the south). This saw even the US stock exchange close as some 60,000 fans descended on the then new Union Course in Jamaica, New York State. The Stevens brothers were said to have bet everything, from cash to their jewellery and watches, on the horse from the north winning. It did and 'The Eclipse' won the day by a short nose with the social ramifications and significance enormous for the times amongst the deeply divided horse-breeding and rearing world.

Stevens's sporting prowess was legendary, and he is further credited with introducing cricket to America – a sport that didn't capture the imagination, whilst on his Hoboken estate he installed a baseball diamond and allowed any club free use of it for games.

After the death of his father in 1838, John Cox Stevens inherited the business interest (Edwin Augustus Stevens ran the Hoboken estate) and built the schooner *Onkahye* in 1839. He then went on to commission arguably the most significant of his yachts, the 49-foot waterline schooner *Gimcrack*, from noted designer and boatbuilder George Steers, in the early 1840s, with its four feet deep and ten-foot-long fin keel – almost certainly the first in the world.

Whilst the *Gimcrack* remains undoubtedly of cultural and historic significance, and we will dig into that shortly, the *Maria*, built by Stephens in 1845 was perhaps of even greater importance. Designed by his closest brother in age, Robert Livingston Stevens, the *Maria* was both evolutionary and revolutionary in its own way with such features as a hollow, single-stick mast, external lead ballasting and, rather remarkably for the age, cross-cut sails that were flatter than anything seen before. Over the course of the next two decades and more that the *Maria* was owned by the Stevens family, they are said to have spent over $100,000 on technical improvements – a simply vast sum of money for the time.

Robert L. Stevens was very much of the same mould as his father. An ingenious inventor who was credited at a later date with the first all-iron rail construction for rail track, but his heart, along with that of his elder brother John, was in boats. The younger Stevens, after a childhood messing around on the banks of Hoboken, was part of his father's *Phoenix* steam boat project and further applied the wave-line theory onto a subsequent steam ship of his own design in 1808, introducing a concave waterline. When his brother asked for the design of the *Maria*, many years later in 1844, it was with an inventor's eye that he approached the project. What was produced was sensational and held for a long while the title of the 'fastest yacht afloat'. This was to be tested most sternly by the formation of what was to become the most famous yacht club in the world.

The wave-line theory is worthy of note in the mid-19th century as the profitability of the steam ships was directly correlated to the coal consumption of the vessel. More resistance equalled less profit, so the designers from the early 1800s were detailed to streamline the hulls whilst navies around the world were also turning to the shipyards and designers for faster sail and steamboats for more obvious reasons. Step forward John Scott Russell who, having studied mathematics at the University of Glasgow from 1821 to 1825, began learning his trade through building steam ship motors alongside steam engines for the railroads. Russell's foray into ships began with a new innovation of the early Victorian age – the steam-driven canal boat – a weighty, high displacement hull that allowed him to develop a theory that has since been debunked.

Russell's 'wave-line' hypothesis was predicated on the theory that the making of a wave relied solely on the shape of the hull and surmised that due to the blunt convex shape of the bow of a ship (or canal boat in his first theory), it ultimately generates a 'wave' that must be continually pushed out of the way by the ship. What Russell believed was that a concave shaped hull, which he describes as 'hollow', would push that same body of water down the length of the hull without creating the bow wave. The British Association for the Advancement of Science supported Russell over the next eight years with a vast sum of money – the equivalent of a million dollars today – to develop ship designs for practical use that would show a significant reduction in wave generation.

In total, Russell built around 100 models to test his theory before proclaiming to have found a new law in physics. Although this ultimately was not to be the case, the theory is still being debated today, as this recent article in *Physics Today* demonstrates:

> It did not provide a way to estimate wave-making resistance; Russell simply assumed, quite incorrectly, that the wave-line hull form had zero wave-making resistance. The wave-line theory also did not have a basis in physics; despite his claims to have performed thousands of experiments, Russell had little data elucidating the mechanism of wave-making resistance. With its insistence on sine curves and cycloids, the wave line was less a physical theory and more a geometrically descriptive concept. Finally, contrary to Russell's assertions, the wave line did not provide a surefire template for every ship. Ship design always reflects a compromise between speed, stability, strength, and dozens of other factors. In the case of the wave line, the need to immerse enough of the hull to counterbalance the ship's weight often meant that waterlines had to be revised away from the pure form that Russell envisioned.

However, for the creation of those first clipper ships in the early 1840s plying the China route, John Griffiths (the notable builder of those early vessels) credited Russell's theory for the creation of some of the fastest sail boats of the time – *Rainbow* in 1845 and *Sea Witch* in 1846. Other notable boats to conform to the wave-line theory included Robert Stephenson's *Titania* and that most famous of yachts: *America*.

At 5 pm, on the 30 July 1844, nine yacht owners, contemporaries and family members met aboard the 25-ton schooner *Gimcrack*, sat at anchor off the New York Battery, and set out to form what would become the New York Yacht Club. It was the day before a planned summer cruise up to Newport, Rhode Island, and the nine men – John Cox Stevens, Hamilton Wilkes, William Edgar, John Clarkson Jay, George Lee Schuyler, James M. Waterbury, Louis A. Depau, George E. Rollins and James Rogers came to an agreement that a formal arrangement should be made, and discussions took place informally for the rest of the year regarding the creation of the club. The minutes of that meeting are recorded as follows:

> MINUTES OF THE NEW YORK YACHT CLUB
>
> *On board of the 'Gimcrack,' off the Battery (New York Harbour), 30 July 1844, 5 P. M.*
>
> According to previous notice, the following gentlemen assembled for the purpose of organising a Yacht Club, viz.: John C. Stevens, Hamilton Wilkes, William Edgar, John C. Jay, George L. Schuyler, Louis A. Depau, George B. Rollins, James M. Waterbury, James Rogers, and on motion it was resolved to form a Yacht Club. On motion it was resolved

> that the title of the club be The New York Yacht Club. On motion it was resolved that the gentlemen present be the original members of the club. On motion it was resolved that John C. Stevens be the Commodore of the club. On motion it was resolved that a committee of five be appointed by the Commodore to report rules and regulations for the government of the club. The following gentlemen were appointed, viz.: John C. Stevens, George L. Schuyler, John C. Jay, Hamilton Wilkes, and Captain Rogers. On motion it was resolved that the club make a cruise to Newport, Rhode Island, under command of the Commodore. The following yachts were represented at this meeting, viz.: 'Gimcrack,' John C. Stevens; 'Spray,' Hamilton Wilkes; 'Cygnet,' William Edgar; 'La Coquille,' John C. Jay; 'Dream,' George L. Schuyler; 'Mist,' Louis A. Depau; 'Minna,' George B. Rollins; 'Adda,' Captain Rogers. After appointing Friday, August 2, at 9 A.M., the time for sailing on the cruise, the meeting adjourned. JOHN C. JAY, Recording Secretary.

On 17 March 1845, the first recorded meeting took place at Windhorst's Coffee House on Park Row, a busy thoroughfare just up from the steamship docks and boatyards of Water Street at the bottom of Manhattan Island. Very little is known today as to why this coffee shop was selected, but as we saw with the 'Thatch'd House' in London where the Royal Yacht Squadron was formed, the coffee houses of the day provided ample meeting space and privacy. The New York Yacht Club was not the first yacht club in America as is so often quoted – clubs in both Boston and Delaware had preceded it, but in terms of effect, it was to become not only a national but global powerhouse that greatly advanced yacht racing and continues to do so to this day.

At the March 1845 meeting, John Cox Stevens was unanimously voted in as Commodore, Hamilton Wilkes assumed the post of Vice Commodore, John Clarkson Jay took on the role of Recording Secretary and George B. Rollins, the Corresponding Secretary. At the meeting, as was recorded in *The Lawson History*, Stevens offered the first official clubhouse described as a modest structure, 'on the level shore above Castle Point in Hoboken known as the Elysian Fields.'

Stevens wanted to model the Elysian Fields on his 700-acre estate into a quasi-public rural retreat modelled on the Victorian landscape garden style that he so admired. He developed it to feature a spa called Sybil's Cave (first excavated by Col. John Stevens III), river walks, fishing and even a hotel called the Colonnade Hotel & Tavern, all served by a pier and dock that could land visitors from the New York hubs of Barclay, Canal and Christopher streets. Years before, in 1824, his father had offered to sell the land to the city of New York as public space for health and recreation, but this was rejected in favour of development of what is now Central Park. Undeterred, Col. Stevens continued the renovation through to his death and passed the mantle on to his sons.

The New York Yacht Club flourished under the stewardship of the energetic and charismatic Stevens who held office through to 1854 before handing over to fellow founder William Edgar who then led the club through to 1858. Following on, Edwin A. Stevens ascended to Commodore from 1858 through to 1865 when the club was incorporated 'for the purpose of encouraging yacht building and naval architecture, and the cultivation of naval science'. A move from the Hoboken clubhouse in 1868 saw the New York Yacht Club move to Staten Island before moving again to the second floor of a house on Madison Avenue and 27th street.

The club struggled in the period after the 'Panic of 1873' which led to the 'Great Depression' with the club forced to rely on wealthy members to keep it alive. As a result the Staten Island clubhouse was given up around 1877 before moving to 27 Madison Avenue where it remained until the banking scion John Pierpont Morgan gifted the land on which the present-day clubhouse stands rather magnificently at 37–41 West 44th Street.

Undoubtedly the most significant period of the newly-formed New York Yacht Club was the period leading up to the Great Exhibition of the Works of Industry of all Nations and the decision to send a yacht for trial and comparison against the perceived might of the British fleet. Although not officially part of the National Institute's efforts towards Prince Albert's Great Exhibition in Hyde Park, on reflection, and in light of what happened at the Crystal Palace and the derision encountered by the Americans in the British print media, the efforts by the New York Yacht Club's foremost members ultimately saved face and created a bridge between the Old and New Worlds.

Historians, as well as contemporary writers, have debated from many angles the virtues of the yacht *America*, which crossed the Atlantic and defeated the Royal Yacht Squadron's fleet. However, examining the 'risk' from the eyes of those that decided to form a syndicate and test themselves, one thing is clear. These men were of the opinion that advances in American shipbuilding were 'light years' away from their British counterparts, who could easily be accused of that most British of characteristics – 'complacency'. It was complacency that ultimately has led to over 173 years of failure at the greatest sailing competition in the world.

In Britain in the mid-19th century, rich men were increasingly starting to build and race yachts for pleasure. Over on the other side of the Atlantic it was a different story. Yes, there were small pleasure craft dotted around creeks and inlets all the way up the East Coast which people enjoyed simply sailing or using for fishing, but the sport of racing in its nascent form was centred around betting and very much not for the common man. However, where the Americans excelled was in the growing clipper fleets built to 'clip off the miles' with three masts, up to 35 sails and slender hulls that may not have been optimised for freight over sheer speed.

The *Rainbow*, launched in 1845, was the forerunner of the clipper fleet built to ply the China trade route from the East Coast and around Cape Horn. She featured a vast sail area which many thought overloaded the vessel, but the 'clipper bow' was the sensation in design with its concave line that bucked the trend of yacht design and she set the record for out and back to China of seven months and seventeen days. It is unlikely that the Stevens brothers failed to take influence from the radical *Rainbow* design or the *Sea Witch* which demolished the Hong Kong to New York route to just 77 days. At 192 feet, the *Sea Witch* featured a 140-foot mainmast and was built to carry high value porcelain and tea from the Orient.

Nearer to home on the East Coast, the Stevens brothers will also have seen and noted the incredible performance of the US schooner pilot boats, which were put to sea in all conditions and with extremely flat-cut sails could go to weather better than any craft. The finest example of what became to be known as the 'Sandy Hook Pilot Fleet' was the gaff-rigged, two-masted *Mary Taylor*, off the drawing-board of then 30-year-old designer George Steers, built in 1849 at the Hathorne & Steers Shipyard at the foot of North First Street in Williamsburg, New York. Where Steers departed from the norm was again similar to the clipper philosophy with a narrow bow that could pierce the waves and a long sloping keel that was at its deepest aft whilst also maintaining what was considered to be an extremely thin beam that was widest around amidships. In service, the *Mary Taylor* was sensational, easily able to outrun the other Sandy Hook Pilot vessels.

For John Cox Stevens and his brothers, already owners of the 1845 *Maria*, the confirmation of the speed of the *Mary Taylor* would no doubt have convinced them that a test against the Old World fleet of the Royal Yacht

Squadron, in the year of 1851, to coincide with the Great Exhibition, would be a risk worth taking. For men who liked, and could easily afford, to gamble, it was an easy sell to raise the money from friends within the New York Yacht Club for an ultimate boat capable of outrunning all-comers.

It was also the case that the feted Steers was employed in 1850, at the busy boatyard of William H. Brown on the foreshore foot of 12th Street, as the foreman in the wood moulding loft. The Brown Shipyard was one of the most prolific and important yards of the burgeoning New York boatbuilding industry, and at its head was William H. Brown, a 47-year-old Connecticut-born master builder, who had served his apprenticeship at the Adam & Noah Brown Shipyard, which specialised in merchant shipping. William H. Brown served his apprenticeship before striking out on his own and, although the exact date of the formation of his business is not known, he launched his first ship, the side-wheel steamer the *Kamchatka* in 1841.

In 1850, the William H. Brown shipyard had just received wide praise for the launch of one of the true wonders of the age, the 2,856-ton paddle-steamer SS *Arctic*, built for the Collins Line to challenge the passenger and mail service monopoly of the Cunard Line. The SS *Arctic* was part-funded by the US Government in a highly political, vote-winning move to divert subsidies that the United States had been forced to funnel towards Cunard for its service. The government also had ulterior motives in the design, insisting that the SS *Arctic* could be repurposed for military action if required. The vessel launched in January 1850 before a patriotic New York crowd estimated to be some 30,000 strong.

Such was the prolific output of the William H. Brown shipyard that in 1850 alone, the yard launched, in addition to the SS *Arctic*, two steamships, and three side-wheel paddle steamers, working with some of the wealthiest businessmen as well as Government departments with an almost unlimited budget.

So it is curious that such an emphasis is made in historical texts on the America's Cup that, in some way, William H. Brown took a great financial risk in the building of what would become the *America*. With George Steers gainfully employed by the yard, and with his obvious working connections to the Stevens brothers, not to mention his reputation in designing fast boats, it is a safe assumption to make that Brown saw this as both an opportunity and a side-project with benefits.

One of those benefits was the chance to engage with gentlemen regarded as the cream of New York high society. Aside from the Stevens brothers, John

Cox and Edwin Augustus, whose business was in steam ships, the New York Yacht Club syndicate of owners included James Alexander Hamilton, a former Secretary of State, and the son of Alexander Hamilton, one of the founding fathers of America. The young George Lee Schuyler, a civil engineer by trade and a graduate of Colombia University, was both an heir to a colonial fortune whilst plying his trade as an investor in the steamboat line to New Haven as well as having investments in the New York, New Haven and Hartford railroads. Interestingly, Schuyler was twice James Hamilton's son-in-law. He married Eliza Hamilton, with whom he had three children, and then, following her death in 1863, went on to marry her sister Mary Morris Hamilton. Mary died in 1877 leaving him a widower to his death in 1890.

Hamilton Wilkes, the first Vice Commodore of the New York Yacht Club and the son of the President of the Bank of New York, also joined the syndicate, but the most interesting of all was the silent investment of non-sailor John K. Beekman Finlay, nephew of John K. Beekman. Beekman Snr. was known in New York high society as 'Theatre Jack' owing to his partnership with then fur trader John Jacob Astor in the finest theatre in New York, the 'Park Theatre'. Having taken ownership of the theatre in 1798, he saw it burn to the ground in 1820 and it was subsequently rebuilt by the Beekman/Astor partnership before another fire in 1821 delayed its reopening. Beekman had considerable wealth through his Sullivan County properties business and one of the finest wine collections in America. Upon his death, John K. Beekman Finlay inherited the lot, including an estate up in Saratoga Springs, and historian Alf Evers has recorded that he 'lost little time pulling corks at a clip that made him one of the most popular hosts of his day'. Beekman Street in New York was named after James Beekman, father of John K. Beekman, and could well be the reason why the first meeting of the New York Yacht Club was held at Windhorst's Coffee House on Park Row, situated at the western end of Beekman Street.

With the syndicate owners aligned, Schuyler was left to do the negotiating directly with William H. Brown and a set of correspondence emerged with the boatbuilder writing to his client with supreme confidence on 15 November 1850:

> Dear Sir, I promise to build for you a yacht of no less than 140 tonnes custom house measurement on the following terms: The yacht to be built in the best manner, coppered, rigged, equipped with joiner's work, cabin and kitchen furniture, table furniture, water closets etc., ready for sea – you are to designate the plan of the interior of the vessel and select

> the furniture. The model, plan, and rig of the vessel to be entirely at my discretion, it being understood however that she is to be a strong seagoing vessel and rigged for ocean sailing. For the vessel complete and ready for sea you are to pay me $30,000 upon the following conditions: When the vessel is ready, she is to be placed at the disposal of Hamilton Wilkes Esq., as umpire, who, after making such trials as are satisfactory to him for the space of 20 days shall decide whether or not she is faster than any vessel in the United States brought to compete with her. The expense of these trials to be borne by you. If it is decided by the umpire that she is not faster than every vessel brought against her, it shall not be binding upon you to accept and pay for her at all. In addition to this, if the umpire decides that she is faster than any vessel in the United States, you are to have the right instead of accepting her at that time, to send her to England, match her against anything of her size built there, and if beaten still to reject her altogether. The expense of the voyage out and home to be borne by you. The test of speed in England to be decided by any mode acceptable to you and consented to by you in writing. Respectfully yours, WH Brown

The inference of the letter is that the Brown Shipyard would be the builder of the yacht, with no mention of George Steers being involved, so the subsequent prominent engraving of the trophy, presumably after Brown's retirement from shipbuilding in 1853, or even perhaps after his death in 1855, that clearly states on one of the Cup's voluminous bulbs in block capitals: 'BUILT BY GEORGE STEERS' remains one of the Cup's curiosities. Indeed, a tiller that was used for the subsequent Atlantic crossing and is displayed at the Peabody Essex Museum in Massachusetts bore a plaque that clearly stated: 'Designed by George Steers. Built by William H. Brown. New York 1851'. The George Steers denotation is far from being the only anomaly in the engravings on the America's Cup over the last 173 years.

Work began on the *America* soon after the letter of 15 November and subsequent confirmation filed back to Brown by Schuyler on the same day, with a completion date set for 1 April 1851 to give ample time for the completion of trials before setting out across the Atlantic. Work though was slow with the yard distracted by commercial work on Vanderbilt projects and launches in late 1850. Although the pace quickened in early 1851, such was the detailing of the *America*, William Brown was forced to miss the deadline and requested more time.

In a letter dated 2 April 1851, penned by Schuyler to Brown, Schuyler wrote:

> Dear Sir, I have this morning laid before the gentlemen associated with me your proposal to renew the contract between us for building a yacht the time for delivery to be fixed on the 1st of May next. The delay has been one of more consequence to the convenience of some of these gentlemen than I had supposed. One of them is obliged to sail for Europe on the 1st of May and consequently will lose all the trials, and another who was ready to sail at that time is obliged to change all his plans. I propose to continue the contract between us which expired April 1st, to May 1st, 1851, as the time for the delivery of the vessel, all other conditions to remain as before, providing you consent to the following alterations in your letter of November 15th 1850:
>
> On the first page, after the words, 'The expense of these trials to be borne by you,' you agree to insert the words, 'The vessel to be at my risk as regards loss, or damage from any source.' The last clause of your letter to read as follows: 'In addition to this, if the umpire decides that she is faster than any vessel in the United States, you are to have the right, instead of accepting her at that time, to send her to England, match her against anything built there which in your judgement gives her a fair chance in a trial of speed, and, if beaten, reject her altogether; the expense of the voyage out and home to be borne by you, and the vessel to be at your risk. The test of speed in England above referred to shall be decided by the result of any one or more trials acceptable by you, and to which you, or some person authorised by you, shall have consented in writing.'
>
> Please answer immediately whether you accept these changes and if you do go ahead without loss of time. George L. Schuyler

The month's delay to 1 May 1851 (the *America* was actually delivered on the 3 May 1851) was reluctantly granted by the syndicate, and the Stevens brothers and Colonel Hamilton were forced to change their original plans to sail the boat over and instead caught steamships to Europe. Here, they waited for the yacht in Paris where they procured fine wines and spirits for the galley.

An interested observer of the syndicate, albeit from afar in Washington, was a certain Sir Henry Bulwer, the rather out-of-favour British Ambassador to America, who had been posted overseas after some disastrous diplomatic gaffs in Europe in 1849. Crucially to this story, however, was the fact that Bulwer was a close associate of the Earl of Wilton, Commodore of the Royal

Yacht Squadron, and alerted him to the growing anticipation around the syndicate and their proposal to come to England that summer as a by-part of the Great Exhibition. Wilton was quick to act and extended an invitation, writing to John Cox Stevens on 22 February 1851,

> 7, GROSVENOR. SQUARE, LONDON, February 22, 1851.
>
> Sir, Understanding from Sir H. Bulwer that a few of the members of the New York Yacht Club are building a schooner which it is their intention to bring over to England this summer, I have taken the liberty of writing to you in your capacity of Commodore to request you to convey to those members, and any friends that may accompany them on board the yacht, an invitation on the part of myself and the members of the Royal Yacht Squadron to become visitors of the clubhouse at Cowes during their stay in England. For myself, may I be permitted to say that I shall have great pleasure in extending to your countrymen any civility that lies in my power, and shall be very glad to avail myself of any improvements in shipbuilding that the industry and skill of your nation have enabled you to elaborate? I remain, sir, Your obedient servant, WILTON, Commodore, Royal Yacht Squadron.

There then ensued a remarkably cordial flurry of correspondence between the two, demonstrating Stevens's ability to successfully play along with the British sense of superiority. As he responded on 26 March 1851,

> My Lord, I regret that an accident prevented the reception of your letter until after the packet of the 12th had sailed. I take the earliest opportunity offered to convey to the gentlemen of the Royal Yacht Squadron and to yourself the expression of our warmest thanks for your invitation to visit the clubhouse at Cowes. Some four or five friends and myself have a yacht on the stocks which we hope to launch in the course of a few weeks. Should she answer the sanguine expectations of her builder and fulfil the stipulations he has made, we propose to avail ourselves of your friendly bidding, and take with a good grace the sound thrashing we are likely to get by venturing our longshore craft on your rough waters. I fear the energy and experience of your persevering yachtsmen will prove an over-match for the industry and skill of their aspiring competitors. Should the schooner fail to meet the expectations of her builder, not the least of our regrets will be to have lost the opportunity of personally thanking the gentlemen of the Royal Yacht Squadron and yourself for your considerate kindness. With

> the hope that we may have the pleasure of reciprocating a favour so frankly bestowed, I remain, Your lordship's most obedient servant, JOHN C. STEVENS, Commodore, New York Yacht Club

America was finally launched on the 3 May 1851 and immediately went into fit-out and trials against Commodore Stevens's newly lengthened *Maria*, widely thought to be the fastest yacht in America. Indeed, in those trials, *America* underperformed, especially in flat water and lighter airs with *Maria* setting a mainsail of some 5,790 square feet and a jib of some 2,100 square feet – in comparison *America* carried a mainsail of some 5,263 square feet. Records at the time, recorded in *The Lawson History*, suggest that *Maria* 'sailed completely around the schooner three times in a short distance'.

Despite the notable lack of performance against *Maria*, the syndicate was safe in the knowledge that *America* had something despite the fact that throughout the three days of trials, 14–16 May 1851, she underperformed her potential. After the first day of racing, around eight tons of iron ballast were added around the base of the foremast and it is recorded that on the third day of racing, *America* retired with a broken main gaff and a sprung foremast. What the Stevens brothers could see though was that in typical pilot boat fashion, *America* would be easily faster than *Maria* in any kind of rough water expected off the English coast, and that *America* was considerably faster than the third yacht *Cornelia*, which also contested the trials. The thinking was that with an improved sail and spar plan, *America* would be primed to take on not just the Atlantic crossing but the very best of the British fleet.

The syndicate, however, was not best pleased with either the timetabling nor delivery and on the 24 May 1851, Schuyler, deciding to chance his luck, wrote to William H. Brown with an offer to buy the vessel outright:

> Dear Sir, So much more time has elapsed than was anticipated by you in completing the yacht 'America' that I fear if delayed much longer by further trials the proper season for sending her to England will have passed. The gentlemen interested with me in the contract I have with you have consented that I should make an offer for the vessel as she is, releasing her from further trials and despatching her forthwith. I will give you $20,000 in cash for the yacht finished as per contract equipped and ready for sea, to be delivered to me on or before the second day of June next. All expenses of trials etc. heretofore incurred by you to be paid by you. Yours Truly, George L. Schuyler

Left with little choice and with a burgeoning business that was about to undergo substantial change, Brown was being forced into a corner. But whether he accepted the offer and *America* was taken under the full control of the syndicate with immediate effect, or not, the New York Customs House Registry, dated 17 June 1851, stated: 'William H. Brown, master, builder, and sole owner of the yacht schooner *America*. Built in New York in 1851. Length 93 feet 6 inches, breadth 22 feet six inches, depth 9 feet, measurement 170, 50–95ths tons.'

How dealings with the *America* unfolded post-delivery, the next day on 18 June 1851, are not recorded in history in any detail, but the assumption is that ownership was transferred before sea trials against the *Maria* and certainly before the yacht set off for British waters. The fact that the syndicate was able to sell the *America* at the end of the summer sailing season in Cowes indicates outright ownership.

The yacht *America* in early sea trials with John Cox Stevens's yacht *Maria* off the Battery Headland in New York, 1851.

CHAPTER FOUR

THE MOST FAMOUS YACHT IN THE WORLD

Yankee Doodle crossed the pond, looking rather skittish. So snug, so trim, it soon was found … That he would whop the British! [1]

What launched that day on 3 May 1851 was to prove a sensation to the Old World, although for the fast-developing East Coast fleets it was nothing more than a logical progression. American shipbuilding and design had eclipsed the world almost unseen, as if they didn't wish to acknowledge it, and all that was left was to prove her speed and leave an indelible marker on the sport of sailboat racing for the rest of time.

The boat that George Steers modelled and then built in the Brown Shipyard, on the banks of the East River in New York, should be looked at in the context of similar designs that Steers specialised in creating. George Steers was somewhat born to the world of ship design having been educated by a shipwright father, Henry Steers, who had relocated his family from Devonshire, England, in 1827, after an apprenticeship at the Royal Dockyards in Devonport and worked as a naval constructor for the US Government.

Reportedly the young Steers crafted his first scow at the age of ten and then designed a super-fast 17-foot sloop, the *Martin Van Buren,* named after the 8th President of the United States (1837–1841), at the age of just 16, which launched his racing career in earnest. Racing against the elite *Gladiator* of the New York Harbour fleet, the *Martin Van Buren,* with its fine-shaped bow, aced the race beating *Gladiator* by a distance of some three miles after twenty-

[1] Sorrel & Perkins cartoon, 1851

four miles of racing in a contest sponsored by a certain John Cox Stevens. The New York elite took notice. Then in 1841 came a most remarkable rowing boat, which Steers had the foresight to name after Hoboken's great watersport benefactor, *John Cox Stevens*. This was some 30 feet long but desperately light in construction at just 140 pounds, and it easily beat the cream of the rowing fraternity, a very popular sport on the rivers, including the *Sylph* and the *Brooklyn*. Steers's reputation was in the ascendancy and a series of pilot boats and schooners followed through the early 1840s before he landed the design brief for the *Gimcrack* onboard which the New York Yacht Club was formed in 1844.

To understand the evolution of the pilot boat class it is necessary to understand the fierce nature of the profession that saw sailors put out to sea to guide in the massive increase in commercial traffic that was arriving to the ports of the East Coast of America. The general rule was that in order to engage and 'pilot' a vessel, the pilot boat had to be first to the scene and this natural competitiveness saw the pilot boat owners turn increasingly to the designers of the day for the fastest boats. This was a rich seam for design and development that afforded designers and shipbuilders the opportunity to experiment with theories and push the boundaries of construction, learning all along the process.

The first recorded pilot boat to be modelled and then built by George Steers was the *William G. Hagstaff*, constructed for the New Jersey Pilots in 1841 when Steers was 21 years old, with a brief to be a faster vessel than the competing New York pilot boats. The feat was achieved and there was much animosity towards the vessel and its designer, but it served the East Coast for some eight years before its owner sailed her to California, determined to start a pilotage business out of the mouth of the Columbia River. Sadly, the yacht grounded on a sandbar on the Rogue River south of the Columbia on arrival and was set upon by members of the fierce Tututni tribe, where it was pillaged and burnt.

However, the *Hagstaff* was the performance profile that gave Steers the confidence to develop and refine his designs further, encouraged by Captain Richard Brown who had been impressed with the handling and speed of the vessel which he commanded out of New Jersey. In 1848, Brown asked Steers for a new model and what was presented to him by the young designer shook his core. The *Mary Taylor* was arguably the most radical design seen in American shipbuilding to that date and prompted Brown to ask 'are you sure?' What Steers proposed was a vessel with a fine, narrow bow (bluff in section) with an equally sharp, narrow stern with the volume at its width. Her shallowest draft was forward up front, and it tapered gradually to her deepest draft right at the stern, by the rudder. Steers proposed that she would be stable and reliable in a breeze – vital for pilot boats that ventured out in all weathers – and laid claim that she would be faster than anything plying the waters. He was proven right.

The next significant boat from Steers was in 1850 with the *Moses H. Grinnell*, which Steers modelled in the design of the concave clipper bow, describing the hull shape as being that of 'the well-formed leg of a woman'. Named after its commissioner, a native of New Bedford, Massachusetts, the *Grinnell* was created as both a pilot boat and to be used for pleasure racing by its owner George W. Blunt – famously winning a purse of some $1,000 in a Sandy Hook race against the *Cornelia*. This was another step forward in design for Steers who concentrated on refining the details of his designs with an eye unmatched for the time. Howard I. Chapelle, the naval architect and curator of maritime history at the Smithsonian Institute from 1957 to 1967, delved into the design in detail:

> [The Grinnell] had a rather marked sheer and a keel rockered forward for over a third of its length, becoming straight with moderate drag aft. The forefoot was cut away, the stem rabbet was formed with a long sweep up from the rockered keel, flaring and raking above. The post was vertical with a round stern above, which formed a small counter. The entrance was long, sharp, and concave. The run was fine with the quarter-beam buttock straight for a short distance forward of its intersection with the after-load line. The midsection abaft the mid-length of the load line, formed with sharply rising straight floor, a high, firm bilge, with slight tumblehome above, to deck level.

This was a radical design for the time, and it's believed that Steers may have been conservative in his earlier design of the *Mary Taylor* in order to establish a benchmark before going full bore on the design of the *Grinnell*. By the time George Schuyler and the New York Yacht Club syndicate came knocking on the door of the William H. Brown Shipyard for a yacht to represent the New World at the celebrations of the Great Exhibition in London, it was perhaps more for the services of its superstar young designer than any other factor. And before we go into the most famous yacht of all time, the *America*, it is worth a footnote that the pilot boat built after the *America* – the aptly named *George Steers* – was thought to be even faster.

American shipbuilding and design were, it seemed on the face of it, a decade at least ahead of the Old World.

Whilst Steers developed and refined hull design, arguably the biggest advances came up aloft in both the spar arrangement of the Steers-designed pilot boats and also, crucially, the sailcloth used. Sailing out to pilot-in commercial vessels required the boats to sail close-hauled and it's here where American innovation came to the fore.

Realising that the British flax sagged and sponged water, the sails of *America* were woven at the Colt's Factory in Paterson, New Jersey, from cotton-duck sailcloth which stretched less than the British alternative. Cut at the Bayles Shipyard, New York loft of Reuben Howland Wilson – the go-to sailmaker for New York's elite racing yachts, and aligned with highly raked masts that angled at almost three inches per foot, the sail-plan was originally for a mainsail carried on the main-boom, a boomless foresail and a boomless single jib. This was, however, altered upon the yacht's arrival in England and a meeting with the legendary Cowes sailmaker, George Rogers Ratsey.

Much historical speculation has been made over the design of the *America* and indeed its overall dimensions. Ship design back in the mid-19th century called for the designer to shape and craft a base half-model from wood. From there, the shipwrights would scale up with a remarkable degree of accuracy to create the vessel in the yard. Unfortunately, the original model of *America* does not survive to this day, but a second model, which Steers had created with the intention of gifting it to Queen Victoria, does. His untimely death in 1856 after being thrown from a wagon precluded him from ever presenting the model.

A large number of supposed at-source dimensions were taken from the yacht at various times, including by the British Admiralty who assisted *America* in dry dock in Portsmouth, in 1851, ahead of a wagered race against the *Titania*. However, we can say with some degree of accuracy that by the original custom house registry in New York, the *America* measured 93 feet 6 inches at the deck level with a maximum beam of 22 feet 6 inches and a stated draft of just 9 feet. The latter measurement has been a source of much debate with the coppering running up to 11 feet. In race trim, post ballasting, this is perhaps a more accurate measurement to those initially submitted by Brown. Her racing tonnage was recorded at 170 tons, although her measured displacement was 180 tons, and she sported a 32-foot bowsprit of which 17 feet was extended forward, outside of the vessel.

To carry the sail area of some 5,263 feet, the *America* sported two relatively similar in length masts at 79.5 feet and 81 feet respectively, and her stays were made of rope with the headstay being a hefty 10 inches in diameter. The main-boom was 58 feet long whilst up aloft, the main gaff was some 26 feet long.

The hull constructions fused a composite of woods with three-inch white oak planking forming the outer hull, which was sheathed in copper below the waterline. Her decks were yellow pine with mahogany coamings and inside the framing structure was a hotch-potch of cedar, chestnut, white oak, hackmatack (larch) and locust woods, braced by diagonal iron straps. Down below she was painted all white whilst her topsides, at delivery, were of a grey leaden colour, which would be finished in France before arriving in British waters.

An insight into ship design at the time can be found in the wonderful description of the *America*'s accommodation by W. T. Porter, editor of the popular (now defunct) New York broadsheet newspaper *Spirit of the Times*:

> The fore cabin is a spacious and elegantly fitted up apartment, 21 feet by 18 feet clear, on each side of which are six neat lockers and China rooms; it contains six commodious berths. Adjoining the cabin are two large staterooms, each eight feet square, with wardrobes and water closets attached; between them and the fore cabin there are two other staterooms, joining which are a wash-room and pantry, each eight feet. The fore cabin is ventilated by a circular skylight about twelve feet in circumference, and it contains 15 berths. Directly under the cockpit which is 30 feet in in circumference, and which forms the entrance to the after cabin, there is a tastefully fitted up bathroom on the starboard side and on the larboard side [loading or port side] a large clothes room. Further aft under the cockpit is the sail-room.

A magnificent addition, that has its own backstory of note, was the beautiful and ornate nine-foot golden eagle that adorned the stern of *America*, sitting atop a scroll of linen, its claws nestling on a stars-and-stripes-adorned escutcheon or shield. A traditional American eagle symbol would hold three arrows in its sinister talon whilst in the dexter talon would be an olive branch symbolising that the country comes in peace but is ready for war. The golden eagle on the stern of the *America* was shorn of the arrows, perhaps a reflection of the gentlemanly nature with which the New York Yacht Club syndicate wished to proceed upon arrival in British waters. How the famous eagle ended up in a public house (inn) in Ryde, on the Isle of Wight, affixed above the entrance door, is a tale of legend, thought to be the result of a subsequent refit in London Docks well after the boat had been sold and re-sold after the summer of 1851. Whatever the real story, some gentlemen members of the Royal Yacht Squadron spotted the crest and arranged for it to be returned to the New York Yacht Club in 1912.

Another wonderful tale pertaining the *America* is recorded in *The Lawson History* and recounts another anecdote written by W. T. Porter, editor of the *Spirit of the Times*:

> Before the America sailed Mr Stevens placed on board two dozen of the celebrated Bingham wine to arrive from the cellars of the late Mr Bingham of Philadelphia father of the wife of the late English Minister to the United States, Lord Ashburton. It was more than half a century old, and the Commodore designed to drink it to the health of Her Majesty. It would appear that The Commodore's excellent wife in 'setting to rights' various little matters in relation to the outfit of the 'America' concealed these two dozen of Madeira in a secret cranny in the vessel so that when he sold her, without this knowledge, the wine went with her. He presumed that through some oversight it must have been taken ashore, and never discovered the mistake until his return home when he immediately wrote Lord de Blaquière, (then owner of the 'America') that if he would look in a certain hidden locker in 'America' he would find some wine 'worth double the price of her,' of course making him a present of it.

With the yacht delivered into the custody of the syndicate on the 18 June 1851, it was a couple of days of extensive, and rather lavish, vittling in New York for the crew who would cross the Atlantic. Captain Richard 'Old Dick' Brown was placed in command; his experience as a co-owner of the *Mary Taylor* and as a seasoned New York pilot was much prized by the syndicate, alongside his unparalleled knowledge of the pilot boat class. It was a shrewd appointment by the syndicate members. Dick Brown, no relation to the shipyard owner William H. Brown, provided the sails for the *Mary Taylor* which at 66 feet long meant that the *America* had shortened spars for the Atlantic crossing and a slightly different plan that included a square-sail and a yard, primed should they be required, for faster downwind sailing.

The goal was the up-and-coming port of Le Havre in northern France which was a gateway port for European immigrants seeking a new life in America. Le Havre had shaken off its unloved title as the 'Capital of Tuberculosis' by 1850, and the arrival of an increasing number of steamships saw the port grow in both wealth and stature. William Mackenzie and the engineer Joseph Locke had been commissioned for a two-year project to build a rail line out of Paris to Rouen in 1841, but by 1847 this had been extended to Le Havre connecting up the capital with what was becoming the centre of commerce on the north coast of France and a vital link to the New World.

A lithograph in the Metropolitan Museum of Art in New York shows Le Havre as a bustling port both as an on/off boarding destination but also as a shipbuilding centre of excellence. Under the directorship of Augustin Normand, the leading shipyard that held government contracts for the creation of warships as well as servicing the steamships that arrived at Le Havre, was the 'Chantiers et Ateliers' yard, and although the precise destination of the *America* is not recorded in the histories of the America's Cup, it is most likely to have been here due to the yard's work with pilot ships, that the *America* was fitted out ahead of facing the English Channel crossing and the summer season of racing in Cowes.

The small matter of crossing the Atlantic, however, lay before the delivery crew of the *America*, and joining Dick Brown was the experienced Nelson Comstock as first mate who had sailed extensively with Brown around New York and would go on to secure fame in subsequent defences of the Cup. George Steers, a revered designer but a gloomy sailor who disliked long passages, joined the delivery team alongside his brother James R. Steers and the latter's 15-year-old son Henry Steers. The number of sailors on the voyage numbered 13 in total for what was to be an eye-opening trip in that crowded North Atlantic summer with plenty of comparative vessels against which to test the underpowered *America*.

James Steers wrote a log, a copy of which is still in existence today, that provided a fascinating insight from both a sailing and gastronomic perspective. The *America* was laden with some extraordinary foods which the dedicated cook was corralled to produce on the 20-day voyage including roasts of turkey and beef washed down with so much wine, brandy and rum that the crew were forced to purloin four extra bottles of rum from Commodore Stevens's private stash to cure 'belly-ache' in George Steers and, it is thought, to cheer his mood towards the end of the passage.

Gastronomy aside, the performance of the *America* was immense – even under the reduced sail, an idea taken up because of predicted conditions in the Solent along with the desire to preserve the boat in the best order for the crossing of the Atlantic. Having cast off from the William H. Brown shipyard, on 12th Street, at 8 am on the 21 June 1851, the yacht was towed out of the East River for an hour, travelling some ten miles, by steamship. Dropping the tow and accepting onboard a pilot, she set sail for the Sandy Hook Bar, passing it at 3 pm. The crew were saluted and cheered on their way by the *Pacific* – one of the first Atlantic cruise liners, which they repaid in style. The first 24 hours of the passage saw the biggest numbers in terms of distance sailed, with the yacht covering some 284 nautical miles (recorded in the Steers log as 'knots'), making an average speed of just shy of 12 knots. What impressed the crew most over the coming days, however, was the yacht's relative speed in a variety of conditions. The log notes that they 'passed a ship with a large cross in her fore top-sail', and later, 'We saw the British bark *Clyde of Liverpool*, right ahead about 10 o'clock, and at 6 pm she was out of sight astern.'

The James Steers log notes that 'She is the best sea boat ever went out of the Hook. The way we have passed every vessel we have seen must be witnessed to be believed'.

As Europe loomed, the pace slowed as the sailors encountered lighter winds, fog at times and some sapping Atlantic rain showers, which Steers recorded as: 'I don't think it ever rained harder since Noah floated his Ark'. Once through, the pace quickened back up to days above 200 nautical miles and, with the wind going forward, the sailors set a small jib and homed-in on a clipper brig that they passed 'faster than she was going ahead'. No wonder Captain Brown said of *America* that she 'sails like the wind'.

With less than 400 miles to go to Le Havre, a fleet of three square-riggers with full sail inventory deployed was spotted ahead, moving in the same direction, and it was the spur that the crew needed to knock off the miles and competitively run down the opposition at a clip. The delivery crew made it safely to the French port, eager to report the performance to Commodore Stevens, Edwin A. Stevens and Colonel Hamilton, who had crossed the Atlantic by steamer some two weeks ahead of the *America*. As Hamilton, recounted later, 'In Paris we took means to obtain the best wines and all other luxuries to enable us to entertain our guests in the most sumptuous manner.'

However, before setting sail and bringing the best of the New World to face the British fleet in their home waters, the stinging media storm surrounding American participation in the Great Exhibition of 1851, by now in full swing in Hyde Park, called for grave warnings to be issued to the syndicate.

The Americans were smarting from their over-promise and under-delivery into their allocated space within Prince Albert's Crystal Palace, and the British media were keen to capitalise on their misfortune. So much so, that before even sending *America* over, Colonel Hamilton was 'earnestly urged' by the then American Minister to France, William Cabell Rives, not to take the boat over 'as we were sure to be defeated'.

These were febrile times for Anglo–US relations, also amplified by Hamilton's journalist friend, the renowned Horace Greeley – a vehement campaigner against gambling, tobacco, prostitution, and capital punishment in his time as Editor of the *New York Tribune* – who had visited the Great Exhibition himself and was taken aback at the vitriol that the American displays had garnered. Greeley visited Hamilton in Paris and is said to have advised the syndicate strongly against competing: 'The eyes of the world are on you; you will be beaten, and the country will be abused, as it has been in connection with the Exhibition.' Greeley further added, 'Well, if you do go, and are beaten, you had better not return to your country.' High stakes indeed.

A ten day, highly co-ordinated and efficient fit-out in Le Havre, overseen by George Steers, brought the *America* swiftly up to racing scratch. Minor adjustments were made to both the stem and rudder, but the biggest change was in her hull colour with the dark, leaden, grey being replaced by a shiny black topside and a smart gold stripe along her hull form. The stowed spars were raised, and the *Mary Taylor*'s sails and rig stowed below whilst the aforementioned lavish golden eagle was affixed across the transom. Paintings of the time don't reflect this, but it's recorded with some accuracy that *America* was 'painted white on her bulwarks, booms, gaffs and top-masts.' The lavish furniture set that had been lashed in place below decks was released and placed whilst the arrival of fine French cutlery, glassware and utensils replaced the Atlantic-crossing fare and make-do galley. With syndicate members Commodore Stevens, his brother Edwin and James Hamilton now in Le Havre, the fruits of their fortnight in Paris were no doubt stored below, ready for the charm offensive they planned in British waters.

The 'short hop' across the Channel of some 126 nautical miles was undertaken on the 31 July 1851 and, by all accounts, did not go quite to plan with the *America* arriving late to the eastern approaches of the Isle of Wight and into a dying summer's breeze that yielded thick fog on the approaches up the Solent in the early morning. The Americans made it as far as the notorious Ryde Sands and, most likely, anchored off the Royal Victoria Yacht Club's beautiful beachfront clubhouse, built in 1845 on the instruction of Prince

Albert in frustration at the Royal Yacht Squadron not permitting lady members and excluding even the Queen herself. However, with no pilot vessel greeting them, and a foul tide, the *America* opted to weigh anchor at approximately 6 am and wait for the Royal Yacht Squadron's expected vessel to arrive and escort them the final six miles up to Cowes.

At 9 am, and bowling down on the incoming tide, the *Laverock* – a relatively new and, deemed fast, cutter of the Squadron fleet, commanded by Captain G. H. Williams of the Royal Navy, came to welcome the *America*. Reports in *The Lawson History of the America's Cup* animatedly describe how Cowes was alive to the incoming of the New World's fastest yacht saying, 'The yachts and vessels in the harbour, the wharves and windows of all the houses bordering on them were filled with spectators, watching with eager eyes the eventful trial.' This was in a speech given by Commodore Stevens some while after the race, back in America, at a dinner at Astor House. It was in reality more than likely to be after-dinner hyperbole as the view to Ryde is obscured most markedly by the East Cowes headland and in the early morning, with fog lifting, it is perhaps a stretch of the imagination to believe. However, what is recorded and recounted by Stevens is that a fully-laden *America* raised her sails and set towards Cowes following some 200 yards behind the *Laverock* in a 5–6 knot breeze and a foul tide:

> During the first five minutes not a sound was heard, save, perhaps the beating of our anxious hearts or the slight ripple of the water upon her [the *America*'s] swordlike stem. The captain was crouched down upon the floor of the cockpit his seemingly unconscious hand upon the tiller with his stern unaltering gaze upon the vessel ahead. The men were motionless as statues, their eager eyes fastened upon the Laverock with a fixedness and intensity that seemed almost supernatural. The pencil of an artist, might, perhaps convey the expression, but no words could describe it. It could not and did not last long; we worked quickly and surely to windward of her wake. The crisis was past; and some dozen of deep drawn sighs proved that the agony [of not knowing if *America* was fast or not] was over. We came to an anchor a quarter or perhaps a third of a mile ahead, and twenty minutes after our anchor was down the Earl of Wilton and his family were on board to welcome us and introduce us to his friends. To himself and family, to the Marquess of Anglesey and his son, Lord Alfred Paget to Sir Bellingham Graham, and a host of other noblemen and gentlemen, were we indebted for a reception as hospitable, and frank as ever was given to prince or peasant.

The Earl of Wilton's gentlemanly hospitality and greeting of the American sailors and the New York Yacht Club to British waters was a remarkable precedent for the times. Satirical publications were, as mentioned previously, cruel to the point of crass about the New World and the most vociferous and poignant of all revolved around slavery.

The famous cartoonist John Leech captured this most accurately in *Punch*, whilst on 18 July 1851, the American abolitionist newspaper the *Liberator* published a letter by William Farmer detailing a demonstration that took place in the American section of the Great Exhibition:

> My Dear Sir, An interesting anti-slavery demonstration took place at the Great Exhibition on Saturday last. The same idea appears to have arisen simultaneously in the minds of [several] abolitionists – the propriety of exhibiting some specimens not merely of hams, locks, revolvers, and firearms, but of the more peculiar staple produce of America – Slavery.

Against this acrimonious backdrop, the gentlemen of the Royal Yacht Squadron behaved impeccably, although the desire by John Cox Stevens to race against the best of the British fleet for wagers was largely ignored by the yacht-owning members of the Club and the following challenge went unmet when posted in the Squadron's noticeboard and issued to the press:

> The New York Yacht Club, in order to test the relative merits of the different models of the schooners of the old and the new world, propose through Commodore Stevens to the Royal Yacht Squadron, to run the yacht America against any number of schooners belonging to any of the Yacht Squadrons of the Kingdom, to be selected by the Commodore of the Royal Yacht Squadron the course to be over some part of the English Channel outside the Isle of Wight, with at least a six knot breeze. This trial of speed to be made at an early day to be selected by the Commodore of the Royal Yacht Squadron. And if on that day there shall not be at least a six-knot breeze, then on the first day thereafter that such a breeze shall blow.

The reference in Stevens's challenge to 'any number of schooners' was expanded in a subsequent communication with the Earl of Wilton on 9 August 1851 to include:

> any cutter, schooner or vessel of any other rig of the Royal Yacht Squadron, relinquishing any advantage which your rule admits is due to

> a schooner from a cutter, but claiming the right to sail 'America' in such a manner, by booming out, as her raking masts require; the course to be in the English Channel with not less than a six-knot breeze ... the distance to be not less than twenty nor over seventy miles out and back, and in such a direction as to test the qualities of the vessels before and by the wind.

It's interesting to note the emphasis from Wilton in all his responses as he barely mentions the promise of 'racing' and he reflected the view that 'The members generally of the Royal Yacht Squadron are greatly interested in testing the relative merits of the different models of the old and new world without restriction as to rig or otherwise ...' And that is perhaps the most sincerely held outcome that Wilton and the members of the Royal Yacht Squadron had intended, whereas the competitive Americans had come for both racing pride and to win sums of money through wagers. In his letter to Wilton on the 9 August 1851, Stevens ended with the words: 'I am willing to stake upon the issue any sum not to exceed ten thousand guineas' – an extraordinary sum even for the more exuberant Victorians and something that James Steers later recorded as being 'a staggerer' to the British yachting fraternity of the time.

The Royal Victoria Yacht Club's regatta in Ryde on the 13 August 1851 was the next logical opportunity for the *America* to get racing, but much to the dismay of the *America* crew and owners, their official participation was precluded due to a club rule that stated that each yacht entered had to be 'the sole property of one individual'. However, spirits were buoyed by the news that the Southampton Yacht Club had accepted the *America*'s challenge on behalf of the famous cutter, the 193-ton *Alarm* – a Lymington-built boat from the Thomas Inman shipyard, owned by landowner Joseph Weld of the Lulworth Estate in Dorset.

The *Alarm* raced in the Ryde Regatta of 1851, and despite not being eligible to enter, the crew of *America* decided to run the yacht with just mainsail and jib, starting behind the fleet to measure relative speed. Even in that configuration, James Steers recorded in his journal: 'we kept up with the *Alarm* with that sail'. Noting the outright speed, no one-on-one match was eventually made between the *America* and the *Alarm* for reasons unknown but suspected.

With time running out, Stevens despaired at ever matching *America* in a trial and perhaps killed the idea stone dead on the 15 August 1851 when again in the Ryde Regatta, *America* showed her outright speed after starting some three miles behind a fleet of both schooners and cutters and overhauling them all within a little over an hour and a half of sailing. Cowes was stunned by the speed of the foreigner, and this was reflected by breathless commentary in *The Times* newspaper with their unnamed 'own correspondent' writing on 14 August 1851:

> When close to her you see that her bow is as sharp as a knife blade, and is 'scooped away,' as it were, outwards till it swells towards the stern, the aides gradually springing outwards, as round as an apple, till a little forward of the mainmast, where she has her greatest beam, being there 22 feet and some inches across. Her stern is remarkably broad and wide and full, affording great accommodation on deck as well as below. She has no bulwarks, at least, they are not above 9 or 10 inches high. Thus, she differs most materially from our vessels, and 'if she be right (as the Marquess of Anglesey said – often attributed to his son Lord Alfred Paget whose yacht Mona was also in the race of 22nd August 1851), why, we must all be wrong.' Standing at the stern and looking forward the deck is nearly of a wedge-shape, or like the section of a carrot, the extreme beam being as I have stated, the bow being as sharp as the apex of a triangle, and the stern being not very much less than the extreme breadth of beam. Her crew are very fine active-looking seamen, and altogether, sail when she will, she is not to be despised by the best boat we have if appearance go for anything.

With tensions running high in Cowes, again on the 18 August 1851, *The Times* newspaper went for the jugular against the British yachting establishment for not having arranged a match against *America* in a lengthy excoriation:

> Most of us have seen the agitation which the appearance of a sparrowhawk in the horizon creates among a flock of woodpigeons or skylarks, when unsuspecting all danger, and engaged in airy flights or playing about over the fallows, they all at once come down to the ground and are rendered almost motionless by fear of the disagreeable visitor.
>
> Although the gentlemen whose business is on the waters of the Solent are neither woodpigeons nor skylarks, and although the 'America' is not a sparrowhawk, the effect produced by her apparition off West Cowes among the yachtsmen seems to have been completely paralysing. I use the word 'seems' because it cannot be imagined that some of those who took such pride in the position of England as not only being at the head

of the whole race of aquatic sportsmen, but as furnishing almost the only men who sought pleasure and health upon the ocean, will allow the illustrious stranger to return with the proud boast to the New World that she had flung down the gauntlet to England, Ireland, and Scotland, and that not one had been found to take it up. If she were victorious after a gallant contest, all that could be said was that the American builder had put together a lighter, swifter, and better made mass of wood and iron than any the English builders had matched against her.

No one could affirm there was the least disgrace attached to us from the fact. But if she be permitted to sail back to New York with her challenge unaccepted, and can nail under it as it is fastened up on one of her beams that no one dared touch it, then there will be some question as to the pith and courage of our men, and yachting must sink immeasurably in public estimation, and must also be deprived of the credit which was wont to be attached to it, of being a nursery for bringing up our national naval spirit to a respectable and well grown maturity.

The discomfiture, I repeat, would be as nothing if we were beaten after a well fought field, compared to the discredit of running away or evading a contest with a vaunting but certainly an honourable enemy. And what, after all, if we are afraid of a phantom? I do not mean for a moment to assert that the America is not the most formidable competitor against which any yacht could be matched; but suppose she has her weak point of sailing, what a chuckle her owners would have over us for not trying to find it out!

She has defied every sort of craft, from the eccentric 'fancy' of the amateur rigger, such as the Brilliant, down to the most orthodox cutter, and her challenge is a loud sounding one; but is it not just possible that though she may beat a schooner or a cutter on several points of sailing, the America may have a failing which a long match in a stiff breeze might render visible to a quick eye in a course round the Eddystone or to Ushant and back? Most undoubtedly it is. The vessel never yet was built that could sail equally well on all points and in all weathers. I trust that, whether she runs or not in the Cowes regatta, her qualities will be tested to the utmost by some of our first-class yachts in a long run.

Unbeknown, presumably, to *The Times* correspondent, two days prior to his copy, Commodore Stevens had written to the Secretary of the Royal Yacht Squadron, John Bates:

> Dear Sir, Will you do me the favour to enter the America for the Royal Yacht Squadron Regatta to come off on the 22nd inst. The fact that this vessel is owned by more than one person is so well known as to render it almost unnecessary to state it; yet I do so when she is entered to avoid the possibility of seeming to contravene the rules of the Royal Yacht Squadron. Allow me further to say in reference to others who may be disposed to be competitors, that should there be little or no wind on that day this vessel will probably not sail. With respect your obedient servant, John C. Stevens

The race for what would eventually become 'America's Cup' was about to begin but so too the rampant and vociferous voices in the media needling the gentleman of the Royal Yacht Squadron into taking on the challenge of the 'stranger'. Arguably, the quote which noted the agitation which the appearance of 'a sparrowhawk in the horizon creates among a flock of woodpigeons or skylarks' was aimed more directly at the club's sporting yacht owners than was comfortable, and it was merely the start of a narrative of invincibility that almost certainly does not stand the test of scrutiny.

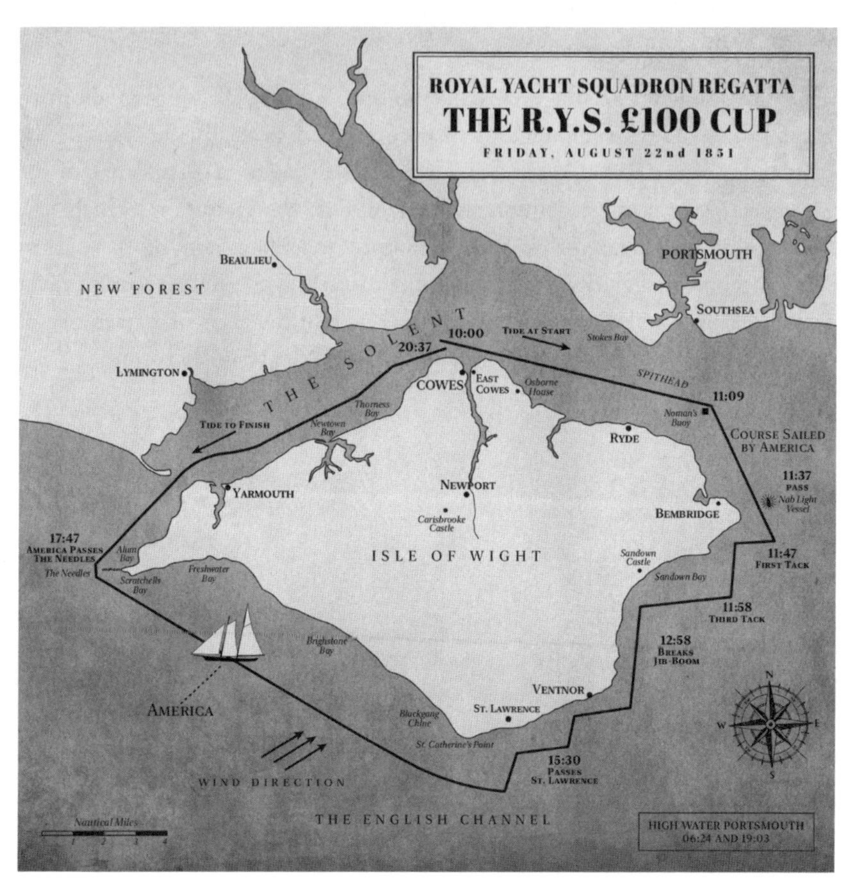

The *America*'s clockwise course of the Isle of Wight on 22 August 1851.

CHAPTER FIVE

THE RACE OF THE CENTURY

The Yankees bein' allowed to crow over the gentlemen ...[1]

With the stinging rebuke to the gentlemen of British yachting from *The Times* column of 18 August 1851 reverberating around Cowes, and further afield, a modicum of honour was restored when Robert Stephenson, the son of the innovative civil and mechanical engineer and 'Father of the Railways' George Stephenson, agreed to accept a trial against *America*. Robert was himself an accomplished engineer who was continuing the work of his father.

That match was to be held at a later date after the Royal Yacht Squadron Regatta, which began on Monday 18 August 1851 with Her Majesty's Cup for the large-class (above 105 tons) cutters of the RYS, followed by the RYS dinner on 19 August 1851. Prince Albert's Cup was scheduled for 20 August, with the RYS Annual Ball on Thursday 21 August 1851 and finally the RYS £100 Cup – a race around the Isle of Wight: 'Open to Yachts belonging to the Clubs of all Nations ... no time allowance for tonnage'.

The decision to run a race 'Open to Yachts belonging to the Clubs of all Nations' was taken at the 9 May 1851 meeting of the Royal Yacht Squadron and is captured in the minutes of that meeting. The intention behind the phrasing was almost certainly not with the New York Yacht Club in mind and was far more likely to have been aimed at the then newly-formed (it was

[1] *Bell's Life* in London and Sporting Chronicle was a weekly newspaper angled most prominently at the horse racing fraternity and described as being 'aimed at the literate poor and the general sporting public that falls into all classes'. It was one of the most critical and forthright publications of the day and a source of accuracy reflecting public opinion in Victorian Britain.

under three years old) Imperial Yacht Club of St. Petersburg, which had indicated, as well as being confirmed and agreed by Tsar Nicholas I, the club's intention to send a fleet of yachts to England in honour of the Great Exhibition. Russia was a well-known manufacturer and exporter of flax sailcloth, but sadly no Russian yacht competed in Cowes that summer, leaving the *America* as the sole international entry.

An interesting side note was the fireworks display which was arranged for the citizens and visitors to Cowes for their enjoyment at the conclusion of the regatta. This had been a prominent feature of the Great Exhibition with regular, and elaborate displays, fuelled by the advances that Italian and French pyrotechnic experts had brought to Victorian Britain in the mid-19th century. They were scheduled for 9 pm on the 22 August 1851 and would have been, most likely, observed at a distance by the royal party from the rolling west-facing lawns at Osborne House over in East Cowes.

Although buoyed by the arrival of the *America*, the annual Cowes regatta had been on the wane for a number of years. The discord at the Royal Yacht Squadron, which had been rumbling through the ranks over the Commodore succession, had led to a progressive and alarming decline in the numbers of yachts willing to come to Cowes. Whilst the likes of the Royal Thames Yacht Club and the Royal Victoria Yacht Club in Ryde flourished, the Squadron was facing an uphill battle for not only relevancy but indeed its very survival – an uncomfortable fact that was picked up by the clawing media.

Bell's Life, known affectionately as 'The Bells', provided a consistent chronology of the Royal Yacht Squadron's in-fighting and perceived pomposity and their net effects throughout the late 1840s and through into the early 1850s. Once, 'The Bells' famously described racing at Cowes in 1850 thus: 'No boats will enter for cups unless filled with their majesties' likenesses', later reported scathingly that:

> The dissensions at HQ were reflected by the very aspect of the Solent, where many Squadron yachts flew ostentatiously the ensign and burgee of the Royal Western Club. The good old days of the regattas have vanished; when Cowes was the focus of attention, when visitors flocked from all parts, when neither love nor money could procure a bed, when Lords and Dukes were content to repose on a carpet with only a rug for a pillow.

With tongue firmly in cheek, this chronicle of the day doubled down on its assertion that the Cowes heyday was over when it published the following:

> We wish that they would send the Queen's Cup to the R.T.Y.C. (Royal Thames Yacht Club) then we would have a race worth recording. The numerous fashionable assemblages did not throng the Parade to witness the departure of the yachts, and those who did go, only witnessed one gingerbread stall and a razor grinder's machine which was placed near the R.Y.S clubhouse. Fortunately, no suicidal act has been committed.

This account is in stark contrast to how America's media, writers and indeed historians covered the regatta. And this is true to the present day. On the one hand, the British writers at the time were keen for reasons already explained to provoke the yachting establishment by emphasising their lack of competitive spirit. On the other, the Americans had a clear agenda to latch onto any lavish description that celebrated the success of the yacht *America* amidst the backdrop of the disastrous fall-out and profiling of their nation at the Great Exhibition. So, it was the British media coverage, poor and often inaccurate as it was, that eventually made it into the history books and the articles of the day.

A great example of this concerned the finish of that race around the Isle of Wight which this author will recount in full. It is well recorded that firework displays historically attracted large crowds at Cowes and could well explain the seemingly chaotic and frenetic on-water scenes that journalists recorded at the end of the race on the evening of Friday 22 August 1851 in Cowes and attributed to the race itself. But to say that crowds thronged both the north shore and all the way down the Solent as the yachts glided down on a dying breeze is surely a most fanciful aberration of journalist licence.

The Times had an even more scurrilous take on the proceedings before the race, aiming squarely at the members of the Royal Yacht Squadron, saying in their 18 August 1851 piece:

> Day after day gentlemen in most wonderful costumes, ranging in style from Dirck Hatterick to Wright in an Adelphi farce, sit at the windows or in the porch of the clubhouse with telescope to eye, staring at the phenomena, or they row around her in grotesque little punts, or go on board and have a chat with the Commodore, his brother, and Colonel Hamilton, three very cautious and gentlemanly persons – as downright 'cute and keen as the smartest in the States, but who can hardly disguise, nevertheless, their pleasure at John Bull's astonishment and evident

perturbation, owning, as he does, a fleet of about 800 yachts of all sizes – from nearly 400 tons down to three tons. At the same time, to show that they are not above taking a hint, they have prepared a jib-boom and jib, and there is also talk of a gaff topsail having been sent on board by Ratsey, of Cowes.

For certain, the competitive Americans, having entered the race around the Isle of Wight, prepared well for racing in water that was famously described as 'notoriously one of the most unfair to strangers that can be selected'. Additional crewmembers were drafted in from the London-based schooner, the *Surprise* that was docked on Cowes Roads for the regatta, but the key appointment was Robert Underwood, a Cowes man, and the brother-in-law of shipbuilder Michael Ratsey, who was sourced by the Commanding Admiral in Portsmouth after an approach via the American consul in Southampton.

As Colonel Hamilton recounted in a speech after his return to New York:

> Warnings of all sorts from various quarters reached us, not to rely too much on any pilot that might offer, and our Commodore was naturally perplexed. But here again the Admiral commanding at Portsmouth, with an intuitive perception of the difficulty told Commodore Stevens that he would furnish him with a pilot for whom he himself would be answerable. The offer was as frankly accepted as it was honourably made. The pilot came onboard, and never for a moment was there any suspicion on any mind that he was not as thoroughly honest and reliable as one of ourselves. Yet so strong was the distrust of our countrymen outside that even after the pilot was in charge the Commodore was warned by letter not to trust too much in him and was urged to take another pilot to overlook him. His own loyal character would not entertain such a proposition, he gave his confidence to the pilot the Admiral had sent him, and it was most complete.

In total there were 21 sailors onboard *America* with the three owners, 13 able seamen, a cook, a steward, Robert Underwood as pilot, a representative from the Royal Yacht Squadron and 15-year-old Henry Steers – incidentally the son of James Steers who along with his brother George had decided to return to New York before the race. It is recorded that tensions around James's consumption led to his and George's departure from the crew with barbed insults thrown later in a journal against John Cox Stevens, but history is fortunate that the young Henry stayed behind as he provided, some 26 years later, in a most compelling speech to the membership of the Seawanhaka Yacht Club (renamed later in 1881 the Seawanhaka Corinthian Yacht Club), a rather different spin on the race and the lead up to it.

Historians have argued about the validity and accuracy of the coverage reported in *The Times* in the form of a telegraphic despatch that was filed at 10.30 pm on the 22 August 1851 and published the next day. In it, a number of inaccuracies and assumptions were made by an onsite reporter no doubt desperate to file his copy as a witness from afar on a steamship with additional reporting suggested from on-land reporters placed strategically around the key turning points of the course. The contested dispatch read:

> The £100 Cup for all Nations was run for to-day, and after a most exciting contest, was won by the America, which beat all her competitors with the greatest ease. The day was fine, and at starting there was not much wind. Eighteen vessels entered for the cruise and went off beautifully at 10 o'clock. At the Nab the America shot ahead, and at the Needles was seven or eight miles ahead of the nearest yacht. She carried away her jib-boom. The Arrow ran ashore at Ventnor. There were no other casualties, though it blew freshly from S-S-W. outside. Many of the yachts have not yet returned. The Queen went off to the Needles to see the race, and the Royal yacht ran part of the way home with the America. She rounded the Needles at eight minutes to 6 o'clock, after which the wind died away, and the rest of the match was a mere drifting race. The America was loudly cheered by all ashore and afloat. The America arrived at the starting vessel at 8.35 p.m.; the Aurora 47-ton, cutter, Mr. T. Le Marchant at 8.55.

Immediately, alarm bells rang regarding the validity of this hurried reporting, in particular, the timing of the *America* around the Needles and the finishing time of the *Aurora*, which subsequently was amended in the Royal Yacht Squadron records; the whereabouts of the Royal party; the 'shooting ahead' at the Nab; and the 'ease' at which *America* won. We will look at all of these points in more detail going forward in the next chapter but one of the most accepted accounts of the race to this day, certainly the one with the most detail at the time, was subsequently published two days later on the 25 August 1851 by the same, unnamed, 'own reporter' which is worthy of publication in full for the context of this book. Using *The Times Archive*, this is the exact wording, some of which appeared at a later date in *The Illustrated London News*:

The telegraphic dispatch which appeared in The Times this morning stated the great fact that the 'America' had beaten the yachts which started against her on Friday for the Royal Yacht Squadron Cup of 100 pounds value in the most complete and triumphant manner; but from the lateness of the hour at which the race concluded it was impossible to send up to town any detailed account of her victory.

It now remains to give the particulars of the event as one of no ordinary interest. A large portion of the peerage and gentry of the United Kingdom who left their residences and forsook the sports of the moors to witness the struggle between the yachtsman of England hitherto unmatched and unchallenged, and the Americans who had crossed the Atlantic to meet them.

All the feelings of that vast population which swarms in our southern ports and firmly believes in 'Rule Britannia' as an article of national faith; all the prejudice of the wealthy aristocracy and the gentry, who regarded the beautiful vessels in which they cruised about the Channel and visited the shores of the Mediterranean every summer as the perfection of naval architecture, were roused to the highest degree and even the Queen of England did not deem the occasion unworthy of her presence. Until within the last few days no Englishman ever dreamed that any nation could produce a yacht with the least pretensions to match the efforts of 'White', 'Camper', 'Ratsey', and other eminent builders. In the Yacht List for this very year there is an assertion which every man within sight of seawater from the Clyde to the Solent would swear to that: 'yacht building was an art in which England was unrivalled and that she was distinguished pre-eminently and alone for the perfection of science in handling them.'

From the Royal Cork Yacht Club which was founded in 1720 to the Royal London founded in 1849 there are 17 yacht clubs in various parts of the United Kingdom – 10 English, 4 Irish, 2 Scots and one Welsh and not one of them had ever seen a foreigner outer the lists in the annual matches. It was just known that there was an Imperial Yacht Club of St. Petersburg, maintained, it was affirmed, by the Imperial Treasury to encourage a nautical spirit among the nobility, and that some 10 or 11 owners of yachts at Rotterdam had enrolled themselves as the Royal Netherlands Yacht Club, but, till the America came over, the few who are aware of the fact that there was the flourishing club at New York did not regard it as of the slightest consequence or as at all likely to interfere with their monopoly of the glory of the manliest and most useful of all sports. The few trial runs the America made after her arrival proved she was possessed of great speed and that the owners were not so little justified as at first they had been thought in offering to back an untried vessel against any yacht in our waters for the large sum of £10,000 or for a Cup or piece of plate.

As the day of the Royal Yacht Squadron's grand match drew near, the entries became numerous and 1851 will be celebrated for the largest number of starters for the Derby and for the £100 Cup respectively that were ever known, as far as I can gather. The conduct of the Americans since their arrival in the Solent had been bold, manly, and straightforward, qualities which Englishman respect wherever they are found and loved to see even in an opponent.

In the memory of man, Cowes never presented such an appearance as upon last Friday. there must have been upwards of 100 yachts lying at anchor in the Roads; the beach was crowded from Egypt to the piers –the Esplanade in front of the club thronged with ladies and gentlemen and with the people inland who came over in shoals with wives, sons, and daughters for the day. Booths were erected all along the quay, and the roadstead was alive with boats while from ashore was an incessant buzz of voices mingled with the splashing of oars, the flapping of sails, and the hissing of steam from the excursion vessels preparing to accompany the race.

Flags floated from the beautiful villas which stud the wooded coast and ensign and burgee rich with the colours of the various clubs or the devices of the yachts, flickered gaily out in the soft morning air. The windows of the houses which commanded the harbour were filled from the parlour to the attic, and the old salts on the beach gazed moodily on the low black hull of the 'Yankee' and spoke doubtfully of the chances of her competitors. Some thought the 'Volante' might prove a teaser if the wind was light, others speculated on 'The Alarm' doing mischief if there was wind enough to bring out the qualities of the large cutter in beating up to windward and in tacking; while more were of opinion that the 'America' would carry off the Cup 'blow high, blow low.' It was with the greatest difficulty the little town gave space enough to the multitudes that came from all quarters to witness an event so novel and so interesting, and the hotels were quite inadequate to meet the demands of their guests.

Among the visitors were many strangers. Frenchmen en route for Havre, Germans in quiet wonderment at the excitement around them, and Americans already triumphing in the anticipated success of their countrymen. The cards containing the names and colours of the yachts described the course merely as being 'round the Isle of Wight'; the printed programme stated that it was to be 'round the Isle of Wight, inside No-man's buoy and Sandhead buoy and outside the Nab.'

The distinction it will be seen might have been productive of larger consequences than could be imagined. The following yachts were entered, the figures representing the order in which they were placed from Cowes Castle Number 1 being the nearest. They were moored in a double line. No time allowed for tonnage:

Name, class	**Tons**	**Owner**
Beatrice, schooner:	161 tons	Sir W.P. Carew
Volante, cutter:	48 tons	Mr J.L. Cragie
Arrow, cutter:	84 tons	Mr T. Chamberlayne
Wyvern, schooner:	205 tons	The Duke of Marlborough
Ione, schooner:	75 tons	Mr A. Hill
Constance, schooner:	218 tons	The Marquis of Conyngham
Titania, schooner:	100 tons	Mr R. Stephenson
Gipsy Queen, schooner:	160 tons	Sir H.B. Hoghton
Alarm, cutter	193 tons	Mr J. Weld
Mona, cutter:	82 tons	Lord A. Paget
America, schooner:	170 tons	Mr J.C. Stephens & Co
Brilliant, 3-masted schooner:	392 tons	Mr G. Ackers
Bacchante, cutter:	80 tons	Mr B.H. Jones
Freak, cutter:	60 tons	Mr W. Curling
Stella, cutter:	65 tons	Mr B. Frankland
Eclipse, cutter:	50 tons	Mr H.S. Fearon
Fernande, schooner:	127 tons	Major Martyn
Aurora, cutter:	47 tons	Mr T. Le Merchant

The mist which hung over the fields and woods from sunrise was carried off about 9:00 by a very gentle breeze from the westward, which veered round a little to the South soon afterwards, and the morning became intensely warm.

At 9:55 the preparatory gun was fired from the clubhouse battery and the yachts were soon sheeted from deck to topmast with clouds of canvas, huge gaff topsails and balloon jibs being greatly in vogue and the 'America' evincing her disposition to take advantage of her new jib by hoisting it with all alacrity.

The whole flotilla not in the race were already in motion many of them stretching down towards Osborne and Ryde to get a good start of the clippers. Of the list above given, the Titania and the Stella did not start, and the Fernande did not take her station (the latter was twice winner in 1850, and once this year; the Stella won once last year) thus only 15 started of which seven were schooners, including the Brilliant (Three-masted schooner) and eight were cutters. At 10 o'clock the signal gun for sailing was fired, and before the smoke had well cleared away from the whole of the beautiful fleet was under weigh, moving steadily to the east with the tide and a gentle breeze. The start was effected splendidly, the yachts breaking away like a field of racehorses, the only laggard was the 'America' which did not move for a second or so after the others.

Steamers, shore boats, and yachts of all sizes, buzzed along on each side of the course and spread away for miles over the rippling sea – a sight such as the Adriatic never beheld in all the pride of Venice; such beaten though we are, as no other country in the world could exhibit, whilst it is confessed that anything like it was never seen even here in the annals of yachting. Soon after they started a steamer went off from the roads with the members of the sailing committee Sir B. Graham, Bart., Commodore, Royal Yacht Squadron and the following gentlemen: Lord Exmouth, Captain Lyon, Mr. A Fontaine, Captain Ponsonby, Captain Corry, Messrs. Harvey, Leslie, Greg, and Reynolds. The American Minister, Mr. Abbott Lawrence and his son Colonel Lawrence attaché to the American Legation arrived too late for the sailing of the 'America,' but were accommodated onboard the steamer, and went round the island in her, and several steamers, chartered by private gentlemen or for excursion trips also accompanied the match.

The Gipsy Queen, with all her canvas set, and in the strength of the tide took the lead after starting, with the Beatrice next, and then, with little difference in order, the Volante, Constance, Arrow and a flock of others. The 'America' went easily for some time under mainsail (with a small gaff topsail of a triangular shape braced up to the truck of the short and slender stick which serves as her main topmast), foresail, fore-staysail and jib; while her opponents had every cloth set that the club regulations allow. She soon began to creep upon them, passing some of the cutters to windward.

In a quarter of an hour, she had left them all behind except the Constance, Beatrice, and Gipsy Queen, which were well together, and went along smartly with the light breeze. Once or twice the wind freshened a little, and at once the 'America' gathered way, and passed ahead of the Constance and Beatrice. Another puff came and she made a dart to pass the Gipsy Queen, but the wind left her sails, and the little Volante came skimming past her with a stupendous jib swallowing up all the wind that was blowing.

As the glorious pageant passed under Osborne House the site was surprisingly fine the whole expanse of sea from shore to shore being filled as it were with the countless fleet while the dark hull of the Vengeance in the distance at Spithead towered in fine relief above the tiny little craft that danced around her – the green hills of Hampshire, the white batteries of Portsmouth, and the picturesque coast of Wight, forming a fine framework for the picture.

As the Volante passed the 'America' great was the delight of the patriotic, but the nautical cognoscenti shook their heads and said the triumph would be short-lived; the breeze was freshening, and then the sprightly cutter must give way, though she was leading the whole squadron at the time. At 10:30 the Gipsy Queen caught a draught of wind and ran past the Volante, the Constance, 'America', Arrow and Alarm being nearly in a line. At 10:45 the breeze freshened again for a short time and the 'America' passed the Arrow, Constance, and Alarm but could not shake off the Volante nor come up to the Gipsy Queen and exclamations were heard of: 'Well Brother Jonathan is not going to have it all his own way.'

Passing Ryde, the excitement on shore was very great and the great ichthyosaurus-like pier was much crowded; but the 'America' was forging ahead and lessening the number of her rivals every moment. The Sandheads were rounded by the Volante, Gipsy Queen, and 'America' without any perceptible change in point of time at 11:00 the last being apparently to leeward. Again, the wind freshened, and the fast yachts came rushing up before it. The run from the Sandheads being most exciting, and well contested. Here one of the West India mail steamers was observed paddling her boat her best to come in for some of the fun and a slight roll of the sea inwards began to impart a livelier motion to the yachts, and to render amateurs, whether male or female ghastly-looking and uncomfortable. The yachts were timed off Noman's Land buoy and the character of the race at this moment may be guessed from the result:

Volante:	11.07 am
Freak:	11.08.20 am
Aurora:	11.08.30 am
Gipsy Queen:	11.08.25 am
America:	11.09 am
Beatrice	11.09.15 am
Alarm:	11.09.20 am
Arrow:	11.10 am
Bacchante:	11.10.15 am

The other six were staggering about in the rear and the Wyvern soon afterwards hauled her wind and went back towards Cowes. At this point the wind blew somewhat more steadily, and the America began to show a touch of her quality. Whenever the breeze took the line of her hull, all her sails set as flat as a drumhead and without any careening or staggering she 'walked along' past cutter and schooner, and, when off Brading had left every vessel in the squadron behind her – a mere ruck – with the exception of the Volante which she overtook at 11:30, when she very quietly hauled down her jib, as much as to say she would give her rival every odds, and laid herself out for the race round the back of the island.

The weather showed symptoms of improvement so far as yachting was concerned; a few seahorses waved their crests over the water, the high lands onshore put on their fleecy 'nightcape' of clouds and the horizon looked delightfully threatening and now the Yankee flew like the wind, leaping over not against the water and increasing her distance from the Gipsy Queen, Volante and Alarm every instant. The way her sails were set evinced a superiority in the cutting which our makers would barely allow; but certain it is that while the jibs and mainsails of her antagonists were 'bellied out' her canvas was as flat as a sheet of paper. No foam, but rather a water jet, arose from her bows; and the greatest point of resistance – for resistance there must be somewhere – seemed about the beam or just forward of her mainmast, for the seas flashed off from her sides at that point every time she met them. While the cutters were thrashing through the water, sending the spray over their bows and the schooners were wet up to the foot of the foremast, the America was dry as a bone. She had 21 persons on her deck consisting of the owners, the crew, cook, and steward, a Cowes pilot named Underwood and some seamen who had been lent her by the Surprise, a London built schooner yacht now at Cowes Roads. They nearly all sat aft and when the vessel did not require any handling crouched down on the deck by the weather bulwarks.

The Gipsy Queen when a little past Brading seemed to have carried away her foresail sheets, but even had it not been so, she had lost all chance of success. The 'America,' as the wind increased and it was now a six-knot breeze at least, hauled down her wee gaff topsail; and went away under mainsail, foresail, and forestaysail, so that it required the upmost the steamer could do to keep alongside of her. This was her quickest bit of sailing, for on rounding the east point of the island it was necessary to beat to the windward in order to get along the back of the Wight.

At 11:37 the Arrow, Bacchante, Constance and Gipsy Queen stood away to the north to round the Nab imagining most probably that it was requisite to do so as the usual course certainly is to go outside the lightship though the cards did not specify it on this occasion. The America and most of the other yachts kept their course around the foreland and by Bembridge. She ran past the white and black buoys at a tremendous rate and at 11.47 tacked to the west, and stood in towards the Culver Cliffs, the nearest yacht being at least two miles to leeward or astern of her. She was not very quick in stays on this occasion, and it seemed she was not very regular in that manoeuvre, sometimes taking a minute, sometimes 30 seconds to perform it. At 11:58 she stood out again to the south-east and having taken a stretch of a mile or so, went about and ran in towards Sandown. The breeze died off at this point, and to keep the cutters and light craft off, the 'America' hoisted her gaff topsail and jib once more.

Under Shanklin chine the set of the tide ran heavily against her but still there was nothing to fear for her rivals were miles away, some almost hill down! While running under Dunnose at 12.58 her jib-boom broke short off. It may be remembered she procured the spar from Ratsey of Cowes, but no blame attaches to him for not only did he recommend Mr Stevens to take a yellow spa instead of the white one they selected, but the boom was broken by mismanagement on the part of the men when straining on it with the windlass and did not snap from the action of the sail.

This accident threw her up in the wind and gave the advantage of about quarter of an hour to her opponents, while she was gathering in the wreck. But it was of little use to them. Looking away to the east they were visible at great distance standing inshore or running in and out most helplessly astern, the Aurora, Freak and Volante, in spite of light winds and small tonnage being two or three miles behind. The wind fell off very much for more than an hour and it was but weary work stretching along the coast against a baffling tide, every moment making the loss of her jib of greater consequence to the America. Soon after 3 o'clock, the Arrow managed to run on the rocks to the east of Mill Bay and the sailing committee's steamer 'The Queen Her Majesty' an excursion boat and the Alarm yacht at once made in to her assistance. They ran down to the ledge of rocks on which she was fixed between Ventnor and Bonchurch and 'Her Majesty,' falling on her with a hawser, steamed away as hard as she could and after some 20 or 30 minutes towed off the poor little Arrow, which won but the other day at the Ryde regatta, in such a condition that 'she never more was fit for sea.' She put about and went off towards the Nab with the intention of returning to Cowes and the Alarm which might have had a chance with Brother Jonathan in a heavy seaway kept her company in the same direction having generously run down to aid the Arrow.

The 'America' at this time was some miles ahead and as the breeze freshened from W.S.W half West slipped along on her way making tacks with great velocity and stood well up to windward. Her superiority was so decided that several of the yachts wore and went back again to Cowes in despair and for about another half hour, the New York boat increased her distance, every second. The Aurora, Freak, and Volante, keeping in a little squadron together – tack for tack – and running along close under the cliffs. This was rather unfortunate in one respect, for, in going about, the Freak fouled the Volante and carried away her jib boom and the boatman's pet became thereby utterly disabled and lost the small glimpse of fortune which the light winds might have given her.

Meanwhile minute after minute the Yankee was gaining ground and at 3:30 was flying past St Laurence towards Old Castle while the Bacchante and Eclipse which had been working along honestly and steadily were about 2 1/2 miles to leeward behind her.

Further away still were visible five or six yachts some hull down, some dipped further still, digging into the tideway as hard as they could and into the wind as well as their sails might stand. The 'America' had by this time got the wind on her quarter having gone round Rocken-end, thus having a tolerable fair course from the South to the northwest up to the Needles, the wind being light and the wind somewhat broken. The persons on board the steamers were greatly astonished at seeing ahead of the America after she had rounded Rocken-end a fine cutter with jib and foresail together – 'two single-gentlemen rolled into one' bowling away with all speed, as if racing away for her life, and it was some time before they could be persuaded she was not the Aurora; but she was in reality the Wildfire 42 tons Mr F. Thynne of the Royal Cork Club, which was taking a little share in the match to herself and had passed the end at 3:40.

The 'America' however bore straight down for the cutter, which was thoroughly well sailed, and passed her, after a stern chase of more than an hour, though the Wildfire when first sighted must have been 2 1/2 miles ahead of the schooner. At 5.40 the Aurora, the nearest yacht was fully 7 1/2 miles astern, the Freak being about a mile more distant and the rest being 'nowhere.'

The 'America' was at this time close to the Needles upon which she was running with a light breeze all in her favour. Two of the excursion steamers ran into Alum Bay and anchored there to see the race round the Needles. While waiting there in intense anxiety for the first vessel that should shoot round the immense pillars of chalk and limestone which bear the name, the passengers were delighted to behold the Victoria and Albert with the Royal standard at the main and the Lord Admiral's flag at the fore, steaming round from northwest followed by the Fairy and the little dockyard tender.

Her Majesty, the Prince and the Royal family, were visible by the aid of a glass from the deck of the steamers. The Royal yacht went past the Needles accompanied by the Fairy at 5:35, but quickly returned, and at 5:45 lay off Alum Bay. The Fairy was signalled to proceed around the Needles to bring tidings of the race and at once posted Ariel-like on her errand.

Soon after the Royal yacht anchored, a boat set off from her in the stern sheets of which were Prince Albert and the Prince of Wales who wore his white sailor's dress and tarpaulin hat. They landed, attended by two gentlemen on the beach under the cliff at Alum Bay with the aid of the boatmen, and it was some time before the saunters from the steamboats who were climbing up towards the heights were aware of the presence of such distinguished visitors. They proceeded a short way up the narrow winding path which leads to the heights, but a wet drizzle drifted before the wind and rendered the walk unpromising and the Royal party soon returned to the beach, the young Prince dancing down the shelving road with boyish vivacity. After a stay of eight or 10 minutes the Royal party returned to the yacht.

The Fairy which had returned to signal again stood out past the Needles but all doubt and speculation if any there could have been, was soon removed by the appearance of the 'America' hauling her wind round the Cliff at 5:50. The breeze fell dead under the shore and the America lowered out her foresail and forestaysail so as to run before it. All the steamers weighed and accompanied her, giving three cheers as she passed, a compliment which owners and crew acknowledged with uncovered heads and waving hats.

At 6.04 the Wildfire rounded the Needles and bore away after the schooner, which by this time had got almost in a line with the Victoria and Albert. Though it is not usual to recognise the presence of Her Majesty on such occasions as a racing match, no more indeed, than a jockey would pull up his horse to salute the Queen when in the middle of his stride the America instantly lowered her ensign – blue with white stars – the Commodore took off his hat and all his crew following his order and example, remained with uncovered heads for some minutes till they had passed the yacht – a mark of respect to the Queen not the less becoming because it was bestowed by Republicans.

The steamers, as she passed on, renewed their cheering and the private battery of some excellent gentlemen at the 'Crow's Nest' opened fire with a Royal salute as the Victoria and Albert slowly steamed alongside the America. On turning towards the Needles, at 6:30, not a sail was in sight, but the breeze was so very light that all sailing might be made to have finished, and it was evident the America had won the Cup, unless some light cutter ran up with a breeze in the dusk and slipped past her. The steamers including the Tourist, which astonished the natives by steaming through the still water at the rate of some 15 or 16 miles an hour, returned towards Cowes and the Royal Yacht having run close by the 'America' under half steam for a short distance went on towards Osborne. Off Cowes were innumerable yachts and on every side was heard the hail: 'Is the America first?' – the answer 'Yes.' 'What's second?' – the reply 'Nothing.'

As there was no wind; the time consumed in getting up from Hurst Castle to the winning flag was very considerable, the American's arrival first not having been announced by gunfire till 8:37. The Aurora which slipped up very rapidly after rounding the Needles in consequence of her light tonnage and a breath of wind, was signalled at 8:45. The Bacchante at 9:30. The Eclipse at 9:45. The Brilliant at 1:20 AM August 23rd. The rest were not timed.

Thus the 'America' made good all her professions. It is with great pleasure that I have to state that a protest which had been entered against her receiving the Cup on the ground that she had not followed the course marked out, was withdrawn and that the Messrs. Stevens were presented by the Royal Yacht Squadron with the well-won Cup.

The bust of Queen Victoria in the entrance hall to the Royal Victoria Yacht Club in Fishbourne, Isle of Wight. [1]

Prince Albert and Queen Victoria at home in Osborne House, Isle of Wight. [2]

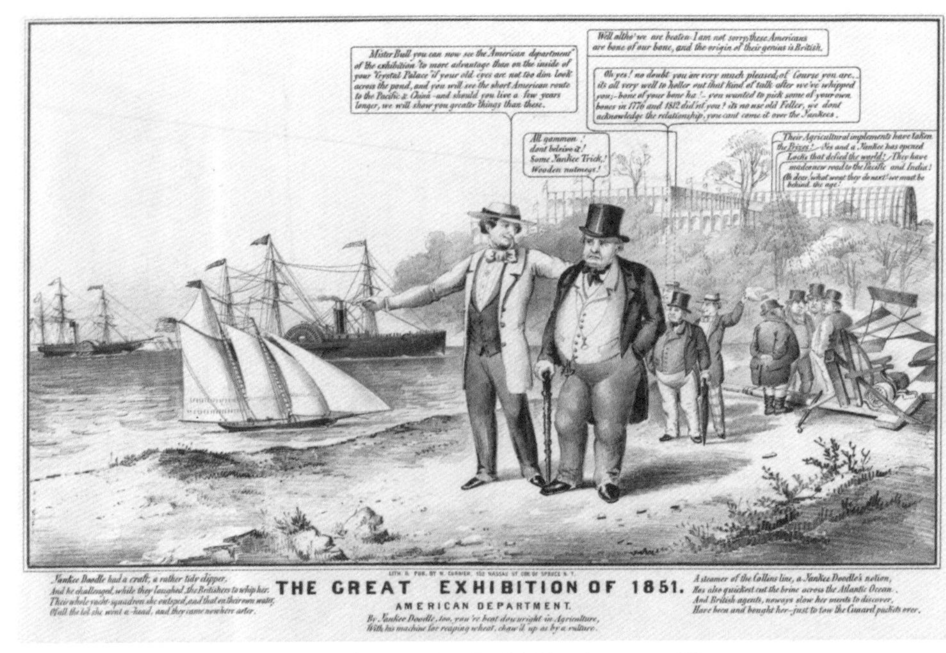

The London Illustrated News cartoon lampooning the British aristocracy. [3]

A view of the Royal Yacht Club's 'castle' in the 1820s looking west to east down the Solent. [4]

The Royal Medina Hotel (originally Drew's Medina Hotel) in East Cowes, the first meeting place for the original members of the Royal Yacht Club (now the Royal Yacht Squadron). [5]

The Queens's Cup Ascot, 1848, designed by Edmund Cotterill of R. & S. Garrard (same series as the America's Cup). [6]

Joseph Paxton, architect of the Crystal Palace, built for the Great Exhibition in Hyde Park, London, in 1851. [7]

The Grand Conservatory at Chatsworth, built by Paxton in 1840 – the inspiration behind the Crystal Palace. [8]

External view of the Crystal Palace in Hyde Park, regarded as a wonder of the Victorian age. The Great Exhibition was visited by some six million people. [9]

Queen Victoria opening the 'Great Exhibition of the Works of Industry of All Nations', on the 1 May 1851, in the main hall, before the Glass Fountain by F. & C. Osler. [10]

John Cox Stevens, first Commodore of the New York Yacht Club. [11]

George Steers, designer of the *America* and credited on the America's Cup trophy as its builder. [12]

George L. Schuyler, author of the original 'Deed of Gift' presented to the New York Yacht Club in 1857. [13]

Model of the *America*, now hanging in the bar at the Royal Victoria Yacht Club, Isle of Wight. [14]

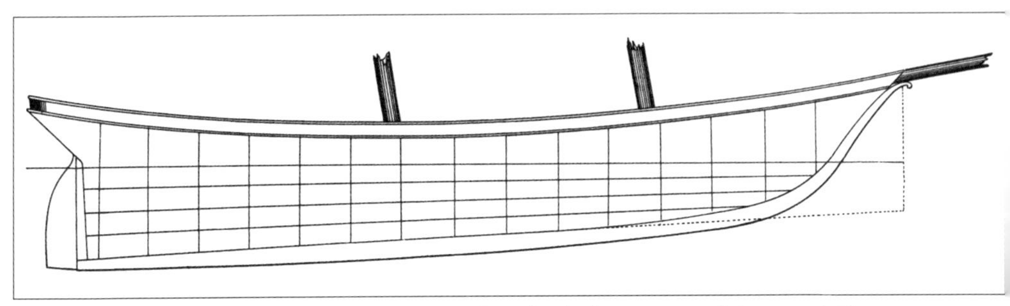

Line drawing of the *America*, taken by the Admiralty from dry dock in Portsmouth in 1851. [15]

The *America* in build at the 12th Street shipyard of W. H. Brown, New York, in late 1850. [16]

Prince Albert landing at the Medina Hotel, East Cowes, with Osborne House in the background. [17]

The *America* being outsailed in her first sea trials against the *Maria* in 1851. [18]

Engraving on the obverse bulb of the America's Cup recognising George Steers as the builder of the *America*. [19]

Osborne House – Queen Victoria and Prince Albert's Isle of Wight residence. [20]

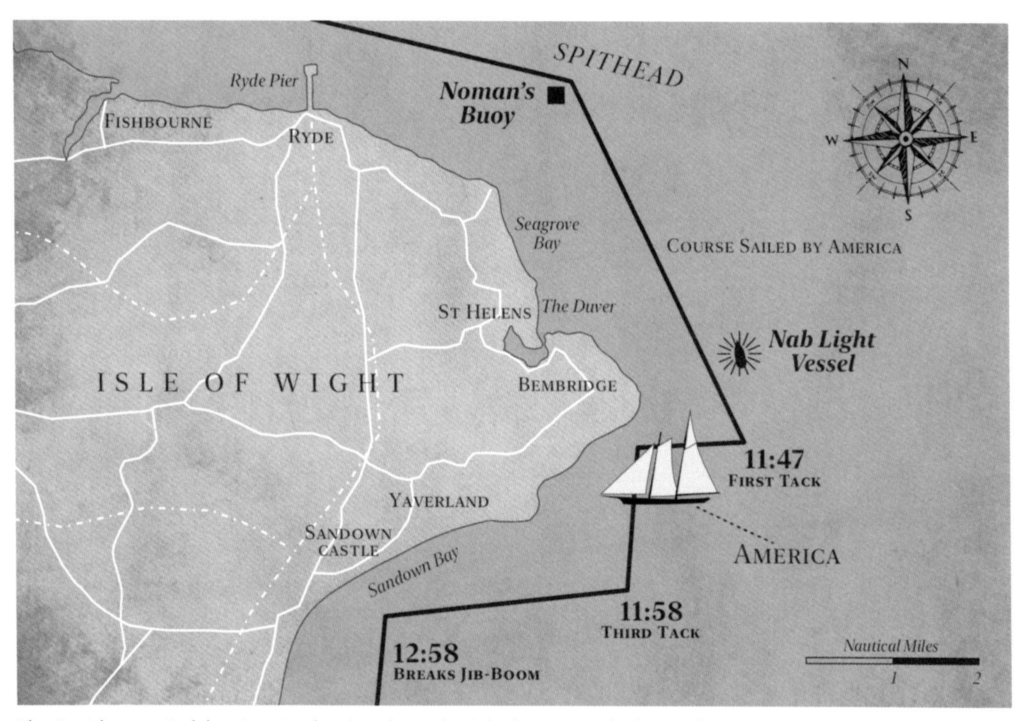

The 'inside route' of the *America* leaving the Nab Lightship to port before tacking towards Sandown Bay. [21]

500, Aug. 1848.

No. 420. 4308

Ship's LOG

OF

H. M. Steam Vessel Yacht Victoria & Albert

FOR THE PERIOD

Commencing 1st of January 18

Ending 7th of September 18

Hand-written Ship's Log for HMY *Victoria & Albert* (National Archives, Kew). [22]

H.M.S. Yacht Victoria & Albert.

Tenths	Standard Compass Courses	Leeway Pts.	Winds	Force	Weather / Barometer / Thermometer	Deviation of Stand. Comp.

Account of the movements of HMY *Victoria & Albert* on 22 August 1851 (National Archives, Kew). [23]

HMY *Victoria & Albert,* from which the royal party watched the *America* round The Needles. [24]

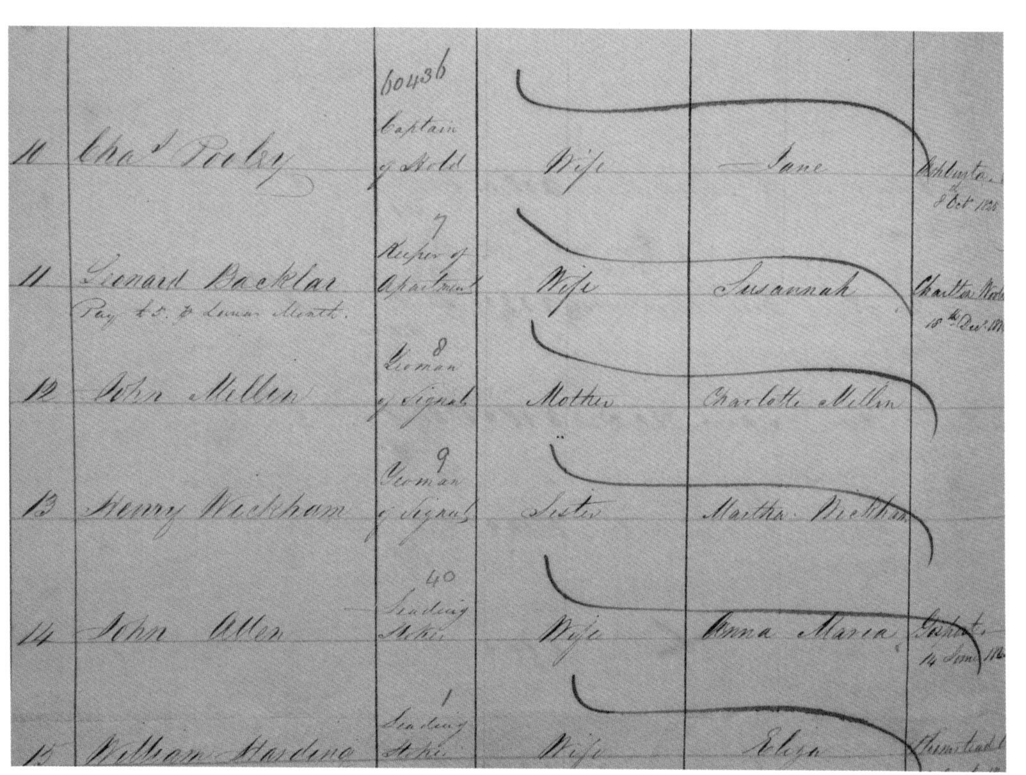

11	Chas Pooley	60436 Captain of Hold	Wife	Jane	Ashburton 8 Oct 1825
11	Leonard Backlar Pay £5. p Lunar Month	7 Keeper of Apartments	Wife	Susannah	Charlton 18th Dec
12	John Mellen	8 Yeoman of Signals	Mother	Charlotte Mellen	
13	Henry Wickham	9 Yeoman of Signals	Sister	Martha Wickham	
14	John Allen	40 Leading Stoker	Wife	Anna Maria	Gosport 14 June
15	William Harding	1 Leading Stoker	Wife	Eliza	

Wage docket for HMY *Victoria & Albert* (National Archives, Kew, London). [25]

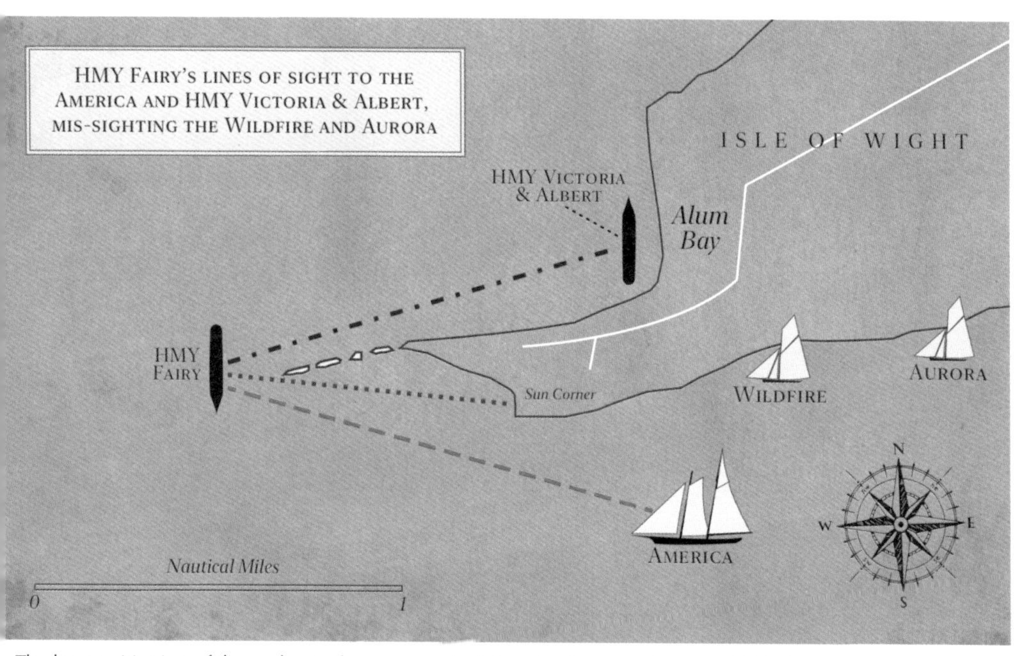

The key positioning of the yachts as they approached The Needles on 22 August 1851. [26]

The Ship's Log of the HMY *Victoria & Albert*, on the day of the race, 22 August 1851. [27]

Detail of the wage docket showing the names of Yeoman of the Signals, John Mellin and Henry Wickham. [28]

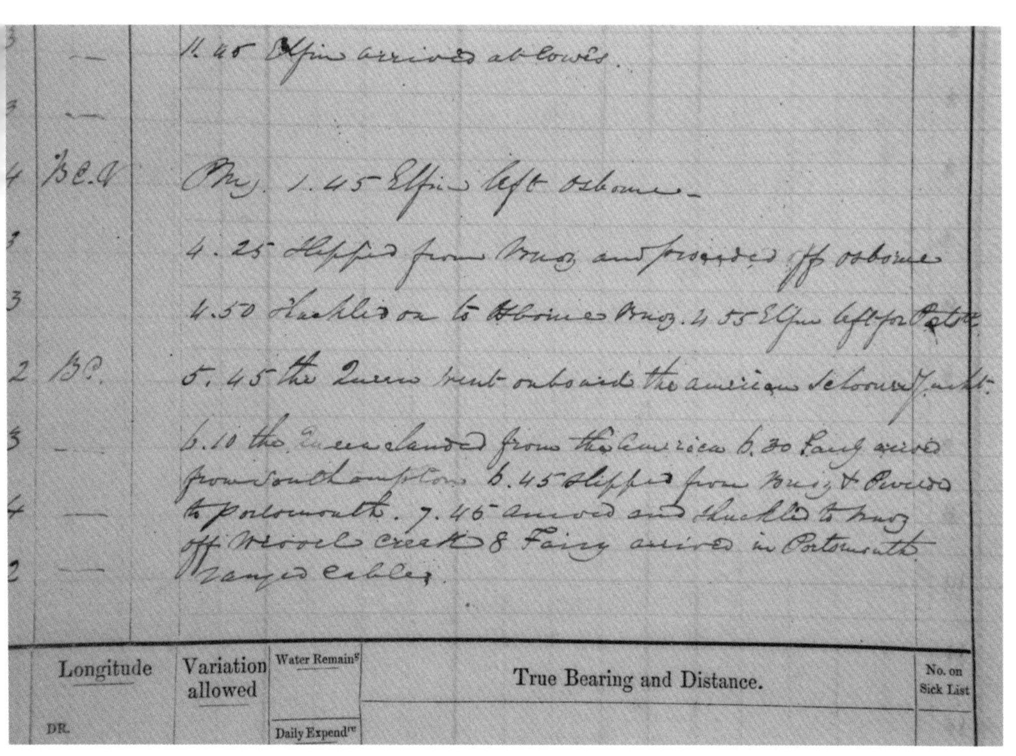

11.45 Elfin arrived at Cowes.

PM. 1.45 Elfin left Osborne –

4.25 Slipped from Moorings and proceeded off Osborne

4.50 Shackled on to Osborne Moorings. 4.55 Elfin left for [illegible]

5.45 the Queen went onboard the american Schooner Yacht.

6.10 the Queen landed from the America 6.30 Fairy arrived from Southampton 6.45 Slipped from Moorings & Proceeded to Portsmouth. 7.45 Arrived and Shackled to Moorings off Wood Creek 8 Fairy arrived in Portsmouth Ranged Cables.

Longitude	Variation allowed	Water Remains	True Bearing and Distance.	No. on Sick List
DR.		Daily Expendre		

The ship's log recording Queen Victoria's visit onboard the yacht *America* on Saturday 23 August 1851 – the day after the race. [29]

John Cox Stevens, Commodore of the New York Yacht Club, greeting Queen Victoria onboard *America*. Note the artistic licence of a ship's wheel – the *America* was, in fact, tiller-steered. [30]

The original crest of the Royal Victoria Yacht Club presented to mark the club's 150th anniversary in 1995. [31]

James Lloyd Ashbury, the first challenger for the America's Cup in 1870. [32]

The American yacht *Sappho* lining up against the *Cambria* in the international yacht races of 1870, starting off the eastern end of the Isle of Wight. [33]

The *Cambria* sailing across the Atlantic to challenge the New York Yacht Club for America's Cup in 1870. [34]

NOT UP TO THE MARK YET.

'John Bull' getting lampooned by 'Uncle Sam' over ownership of 'America's Cup', c. 1893 – a rivalry that lasts to this day. [35]

James Gordon Bennett, offshore sailor and owner of *The New York Herald* newspaper. [36]

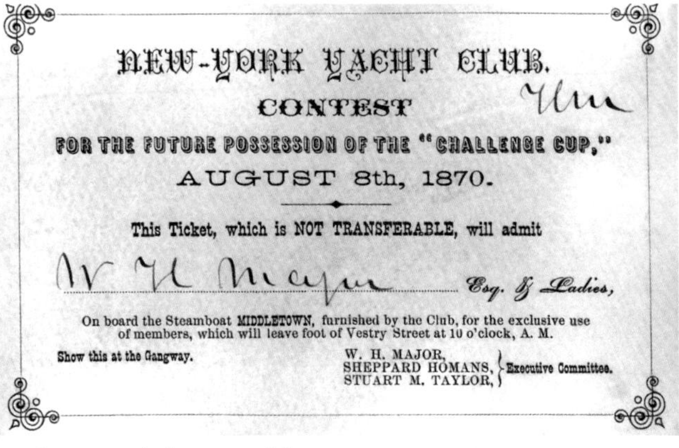

NEW-YORK YACHT CLUB.

CONTEST

FOR THE FUTURE POSSESSION OF THE "CHALLENGE CUP,"

AUGUST 8th, 1870.

This Ticket, which is NOT TRANSFERABLE, will admit

W H Major Esq. & Ladies,

On board the Steamboat MIDDLETOWN, furnished by the Club, for the exclusive use of members, which will leave foot of Vestry Street at 10 o'clock, A. M.

Show this at the Gangway.

W. H. MAJOR,
SHEPPARD HOMANS,
STUART M. TAYLOR, } Executive Committee.

A ticket to watch the races of the 1870 America's Cup. [37]

The fleet sailing back into New York harbour in the first race for America's Cup in 1870. [38]

JAMES ASHBURY 19

THE WILL AND TESTAMENT of JAMES ASHBURY now residing at 7 Old Burlington Street London W, and formerly of Manchester and Brighton I hereby bequeath all clothing of every kind and description to Joseph Lloyd of 133 Leonards Gate Lancaster and all jewelry I possess to W Mc Candlish C.E. of 32 Chiche le Road Cricklewood N.W. My family portraits I bequeath to Miss Anne Smith hereinafter mentioned and all other water colours oil paintings engravings &c, &c, to be divided among my executors as they may agree upon among themselves The executors of my late esteemed friend Christopher J. Schofield J.P. Whalley Range Manchester (he died on o about 6 Jan.1892) dishonourably repudiate any legal or moral liability to give effect to honourable understandings which existed between myself and the said C.J.Schofield to continue to make advances on my securities which have facial or other value of abou t £130,000. and on which he acted in all good faith from 7 Sep, 1889 up to within about two days of his death Within twenty four hours of his death one of the executors hint d to me that complications might arise by such death meaning that no further advances would be made and at such time they were in absolute ignorance as to the nature or va ue of the securities nominally sold on 7th Sep. 1889 to C.J.Schofield to be held in trust for me and for the purpose of nursing the said securities and redeeming them by a sal

The last Will and Testament of James Lloyd Ashbury who died leaving just £400 in his estate. [39]

On the evening after the race there was a very brilliant and effective display of fireworks by land and water along the clubhouse esplanade at which 6000 or 7000 persons were present. A reunion took place at the clubhouse and the occasion was taken of Mr Abbott Lawrence's presence to compliment him on the success of his countryman. His Excellency acknowledged the kindness in suitable terms and said that though he could not but be proud of the triumph of his fellow citizens, he still felt it was but the children giving a lesson to the father. If the America was purchased here, they would nevertheless try to build something better in New York so as to best even her.

The last remark of His Excellency alluded to a rumour that an offer had been made to buy the 'America' but that the sum was not considered sufficient. We have thus been undeniably beaten, but we have been beaten with a good grace and our conquerors are the first to admit it. They speak in the highest terms of the condescension and kindness of the aristocracy they had been taught to believe arrogant and unbending and acknowledge in the warmest way the affability and courtesy of the gentry and of the various clubs.

This evening the 'America' sailed from Cowes to Osborne, in consequence of an invitation that the Queen wished to inspect her. The Victoria and Albert also dropped down to Osborne.

At a quarter to 6 the Queen embarked in the state barge, accompanied by His Royal Highness Prince Albert and suite, and on nearing the 'America' the national colours of that vessel were dipped out of respect to Her Majesty and raised again when Her Majesty had proceeded on board. Her Majesty made a close inspection of the 'America' attended by Commodore Stevens, Colonel Hamilton, and the officers of the yacht. The Queen remained onboard half an hour and expressed great admiration of the general arrangements and character of this famous schooner. On Her Majesty leaving, the American colours were again dipped, and Her Majesty proceeded in the barge to Osborne, where she arrived at half past 6 o'clock.

The very fact that the above appeared in *The Lawson History*, in full, is telling. Much of what *The Times* correspondent reported, most eloquently and with rich detail and lavish wording, can be allocated towards the desire to create and give a worthy account. As we have seen in previous articles, the role of the Cowes Correspondent for *The Times* covered a wide social and sporting brief with often barbed attacks on the establishment but could also laden its prose and embellish with some degree of journalist licence.

A further interesting account of the race was recorded by a speech made sometime later by Commodore Stevens, following his return to New York, at a lavish dinner where the Queen, the President and the Earl of Wilton all received toasts. It is worthy of recount here:

> In the race for the Queens Cup [an error, the RYS £100 Cup was never a Queen's Cup] there were I think 17 entries most of which I believe started. In addition to them there were 70 or 80 or perhaps 100 underway in and about the harbour and such another sight no other country, save England can furnish. Our directions from the sailing committee were simple and direct: we were to start from the flagship at Cowes, keep the No Man's buoy on the starboard hand, and from thence make the best of our way round the island to the flagship from which we started. We got off before the wind and in the midst of a crowd that we could not get rid of for the first eight or nine miles; a fresh breeze then sprang up that cleared us from our hangers-on and sent us rapidly ahead of every yacht in the squadron. At the Needles there was not a yacht in sight that started with us. After passing the Needles we were overtaken by the Royal Steam Yacht Victoria and Albert with Her Majesty and her family on board, who had come down to witness the trial of speed between the models adopted by the Old world and those of the new. As the steamer slowly passed us, we had the gratification of tendering our homage to the Queen after the fashion of her own people, by taking off our hats and dipping our flags. At this time, the wind had fallen to a light breeze, and we did not arrive at the flagship until dark. I could not learn correctly at what time, or in what order, the others arrived.

However, looking again at this race, through the prism of fact and analysis, with a modicum of local knowledge and assumptions of the waters on which the race was run, it is worthy of a deeper investigation. Many anomalies are thrown up and *facts* that have been accepted and recounted ever since are worthy of challenge.

The positioning of the boats around the racecourse is of much debate, the finishing place of the beach yawl *Wildfire* (although not officially entered as she had shifting ballast arrangements not favoured or encouraged by the

Royal Yacht Squadron) and the timings around the Needles at the western approaches to the Solent are almost certainly not accurate.

The debate about the Nab Lightship miss by not only the *America* but the majority of the fleet, and the position of that marker buoy and its net effect on the advantage that the *America* may have scored, are compelling reasons to look again at this race. Equally important are the actual finishing times, after the slow run down to the finish marker boat off the Cowes Castle, amidst the hub-bub of a fireworks night display.

Its wider effects in a socio-political sense are endlessly fascinating. The first race for what would become 'America's Cup' was far more than just a race for an ugly bottomless ewer.

As the skies grey and darken, the yacht *America* crosses a line between the RYS 'castle' and a marker boat at 8.37pm to win the 'RYS £100 Cup' on 22 August 1851.

CHAPTER SIX

THE RYS £100 CUP – DEBUNKING THE MYTHS

There was an awful crying and moaning about Cowes that night we finished [1]

To contextualise the narrative of *America*'s win in the RYS £100 Cup race, a number of factors play into the overall subsequent packaging and presentation of the race itself. The negativity around American participation in the Great Exhibition and the lampooning that the country received, particularly around the issue of slavery, most certainly hurt and shamed its politicians, officials and those charged with attending and provisioning the exhibition in the over-booked space that the Americans occupied.

The race around the Isle of Wight could thus be viewed as a modicum of good news for the Americans to latch onto – especially with a growing shipbuilding interest on the East Coast. Beating the British, undoubtedly regarded as the premier sailing and naval nation, was a feather in the cap to be celebrated and it duly was and still is today, in some quarters. Furthermore, the nature of nautical journalism, as we have seen in the stinging rebuke to the British yachting establishment for not taking up the challenge of John Cox Stevens, was still very much in mind when the wildly celebratory, and almost certainly over-egged, copy was written in *The Times* newspaper on the 25 August 1851. Stevens, of course, may well have been bluffing hard by issuing bets that were eye-watering sums even for the most monied individuals in Britain,

[1] Quote from Henry Steers who was just 15 years old when he sailed aboard *America* in 1851, taken from a speech given at the Seawanhaka Yacht Club in 1877.

The Times, and indeed other London newspapers and journals, it can be evidenced, saw the race as another chance to poke the establishment. This was especially so in the wake of the debacle of the Royal Yacht Squadron's selection of a new Commodore and the subsequent refusal to entertain trials against *America*.

A 'Cowes Correspondent' of the day was expected to do more than just comment on sailing races, with a much wider, and arguably more important, remit to cover court movements, hence why so much prose is given to the whereabouts of the Royal Yacht, Queen Victoria, Prince Albert and indeed the young Prince of Wales. Whilst the royal party was reflected in the most positive and revered manner, the gloves were somewhat off for the establishment in the liberal media.

The underlying narrative of the full and final report in *The Times*, which was subsequently followed up by letters to the editor of great length fawning at the superiority of the *America*'s form and sail-plan, was one that played into the belief that *America* was indeed the rocket-ship of portrayal and way in advance of anything that the British could offer.

The Marquess of Anglesey's presumed prescient comment on *America*, 'If she be right, why, we must all be wrong' is a theory that is well worth testing in analysis of the race. Even the provenance and certainly the articulation and intended nuance of this quote, repeated now for almost two centuries, is debatable. An argument could be made that the inference was jocular, scorning, dismissive even, rather than the reverence that has been recanted by American publications with their very clear agenda. For a while, the quote itself was attributed to the Marquess's son, Lord Alfred Paget, and there has been debate as to whether it was uttered before or after the race. The annals of history are clouded on this key phrase and the exact etymology cannot be verified.

On hull form and sail plan, it is incredibly easy to fall into the accepted narrative, heavily promoted by American publications, which latched onto any sign, quote or signal that the *America* evinced superiority. The pilot cutter class plying the New York and New Jersey routes was certainly refined but more out of need than by conspicuous design. These boats were fast to windward and just off the beam, especially in a blow, and with their under-canvassed sail plan could set to sea in any weather. The flat-cut of the *America*'s cloth and the demand before the race that she should boom out indicated a downwind deficiency almost certainly known and acknowledged by Stevens and his captain, Dick Brown. In a race such as that around the diamond-shaped Isle of Wight, this meant that the *America* would have to fight for every inch to keep the lightweight, 40-foot English cutters at bay, especially if it went light and against the tide. That the *America* was under-canvassed was later proven by her racing record in British waters after the race, and it was almost certainly a miscalculation of Steers and Stevens, borne from the legend of Solent and coastal waters being incessantly rough and windy (perhaps true in winter), that she featured such a reduced sail area.

It is worth noting that when *America* raced in 1851, the sail plan was measured at 5,200 square feet, set upon her racing spars, an area that had been reduced by 12 feet before leaving New York for the Atlantic crossing. However, after she was sold, successive owners increased that size considerably, and some 30 years later, it is recorded that her sail plan measured a considerable 12,000 square feet. This was over double that with which she raced around the Isle of Wight in 1851, as subsequent owners desperately tried to increase the power of the yacht across a wide range of conditions against a rapid British fleet.

In 1851, her hull lines were squarely on the Scott Russell wave-line theory that first featured on the 'wave' way back in 1835. But the narrative that she was fast was established from the moment she arrived in British waters, and this legend was only enhanced by the initial outing against the *Laverock* for the short, ultra-light weather sail from Ryde to Cowes with a fast flowing flood tide. A suspicious and fearing yachting fraternity in Cowes perhaps over-hyped her potency, whilst the establishment, with the means to take on the numerous challenges posed, was almost certainly spooked by the very large sums that the Americans were willing to stake on the outcomes of those challenges. Being astute, and indeed perfectly described as 'cute, the gambler's instinct in John Cox Stevens was piqued and played squarely into the narrative being proposed by the British media. To keep the air of invincibility, Stevens chose the races and the conditions to show his hand but kept the monetary stakes so high for any trial of speed (or race) that, in the summer of 1851, nobody dared to take on the *stranger*.

What is well documented is the starting procedure for the race with all 15 boats lined up at 10 am in two rows running south to north, at a distance of somewhere between 180 and 275 metres apart, with the cutters in the forward line facing eastwards and the schooners and brigantines in the second line. The tide times for the day were High Water Portsmouth at 6.24 am and 7.03 pm. With the adverse east-to-west tide, which at over three-and-a-half hours after High Water would have been running at anything up to 1.6 knots against, quite how the *America* 'ran over' her anchor repeatedly as they hauled up sails at 9.55 am and then weighed anchor at 10 am is something of a mystery. This may indicate a slightly more westerly breeze than was reported in *The Times* if she were to be swung around at anchor to eventually start the race facing westwards.

After her slow start, the quick progress that the *America* made down to the Noman's turning buoy, which was left to starboard, before heading up the eastern side of the Isle of Wight towards Bembridge Ledge, is again well documented. That she faced a blanket of boats ahead of her including the *Volante, Freak, Aurora* and *Gipsy Queen,* all sailing boom to boom, was perhaps the underlying reason for the sheer away to a course that discounted the Nab Lightship but made enough room for the Bembridge Ledge to be safely navigated, and all within a more favourable tidal stream. It was a racer's move, borne of frustration.

And it's a story that exercises beaten British yachtsmen in the race even to this day. The navigational miss of the Nab Lightship, called by Robert Underwood, the British navigator, and agreed by Dick Brown, the skipper of *America,* went by the issued instructions of the day given to each yacht. But it ignored established seafaring and what at the time was gentlemanly convention – an unwritten rule of racing in the mid-19th century.

The exact location of the Nab Lightship has been argued over by many historians and is understandably clouded by the present-day position of the Nab Tower, towed into its current position in 1920, that guides commercial vessels to the eastern approaches to the Solent.

Looking at modern-day charts, both the Nab Rock and the Outer Nab Rock lay a considerable distance further inshore than where the current Nab Tower is situated. If the Nab Lightship (which was almost certainly manned) had been positioned just to the east of the Outer Nab Rock, outside what is called the 'New Grounds' today, this would put the mark no more than 2.5 nautical miles south-east of the Bembridge Ledge marker buoy. This was a non-negotiable object to avoid for all vessels in the race.

Indeed, some modern analysis of the race puts the Nab Lightship as being on, or very near, the Nab Rock. If this were the case, the advantage gained by *America,* and certainly others in the fleet that followed her on this inshore course, would have been far smaller than has previously been expressed.

After the race, as is recorded, the owner of the 392 ft schooner *Brilliant* – George Holland Ackers – protested, claiming that they were 'the only' finisher who went around the Nab Lightship. This claim has been disputed by other owners, but it's clear that several of the yachts – including most likely the cutters *Aurora* and *Freak* – will have followed the course of the *America*.

The decision to cut inside the Nab Lightship is often explained by the confusion between the publicly printed and privately issued sailing instructions. The public version stated that the course was to be around Noman's Buoy (a marker to the east of Ryde) where accurate timings were taken and reported in *The Times*, and explicitly the Nab Lightship, but the private instructions given to all the navigators left out this last instruction. Although it was commonplace to leave a mark to the outer side on a course, something that was certainly a seamanship rule at the Royal Yacht Squadron, the fact that the course card didn't mention it meant that the Ackers protest after the race would have been summarily dismissed had it not been honourably withdrawn.

Henry Steers's speech to the Seawanhaka Yacht Club, in 1877, gave a further interesting insight into this key point of the race, showing just how close the British fleet and the *America* were as they entered this 'turning point':

> By the time we got to the Nab (12 miles) we had walked through the whole fleet except for Beatrice, Aurora, Volante and Arrow. We were running wing and wing, and these boats would steer close together so that when we tried to get through them, we could not without fouling and had to keep cutting and shearing about very often being very near gybing.

In those close quarters, and with an effective wall of sail before them, the *America*'s option to take their sterns and head upwind to Bembridge Ledge buoy on a course of 155 degrees, whilst the others sailed towards the Nab Lightship on a course of approximately 115 degrees, and crucially out of the adverse tidal flow, certainly gave her an advantage.

In Steers's recollections were included some interesting anecdotes on the disappointment that the *America*'s crew felt when they were not challenged and therefore did not win the expected 'pots' that they desired:

> From the Nab to St. Catherine's the wind was ahead (it had shifted to SSW and was a variable strength) and there we left them so fast that when we got down to the point, there was not a yacht in sight. Here we

caught the tide and for a long time made little way beating against it and the little Aurora came up pretty near to us and the Arrow was just behind her. After getting by St. Catherine's Point, we had a leading wind, and we went from there to the Needles at a rate of 13 or 14 knots. Off St. Catherine's we lost our jib boom and I remember that Dick Brown said that he was 'damned glad it was gone' as he didn't believe in carrying a flying jib to windward. We arrived at Cowes about 8:00.

We were rigged (on arrival) pilot-boat fashion, no fore-top-mast and no flying jib-boom, and, as we thought we could do better with a flying-jib, we went to Michael Ratsey, at the Isle of Wight, to get him to make the spar. My uncle [George Steers] bet him the price of that jib-boom that we could beat any boat he could name. He named the Beatrice. Then we went to a sail-maker to have a flying-jib made, and we bet the price of this sail on the race. We heard that there was someone in Southampton who wanted to bet, and some of the party went there. He wanted to 'book it,' as they do over there; but our party had no bank account, no letters of credit; all our money was in a bag aboard the yacht, and we wanted the money put up, so this wager fell through. So all we got on the race was the price of the jib-boom and the sail.

What the young Steers failed to mention in his speech was that a certain privateer yacht, which wasn't fully entered to the race, had decided to sail the course and test her speed against the *America*. This was a 62-foot sand-ballasted cutter named *Wildfire* and the excellent historian A. E. Reynolds Brown published a wonderful piece of analysis, back in 1980, titled *The Phoney Fame of the Yacht America and the America Cup* where he debunked the theory, at length, that the *America* was such the all-conquering vessel of legend. It is worth recounting the *Wildfire* episode in full for context:

The 62-foot cutter *Wildfire* was not racing officially. A leading article in *The Field* in 1885 says that after No Mans buoy when all the rest of our yachts sailed towards the Nab she kept right after *America* after Bembridge Ledge when they came on the wind she started to gain and was level with *America* off Sandown. When *America* came under the Lee of Shanklin Down where the wind was lighter and set her topsail and outer jib. The jib boom broke before long due to clumsy handling her Master said she sailed better without it; it was never replaced.

After clearing Dunnose, *America* came into the full force of the flood tide and tried following *Wildfire* tacking in the slacker tide near the shore, but she was too slow in stays to benefit from it, so she made a long tack offshore. It has been said that *America* lost a lot by this as besides the slacker tide inshore, the wind would be freer as it tends to cross the shore at right angles. However, the general experience on that bit of coast is that as often as not the cliffs deflect the wind more parallel to the shoreline making it a dead noser inshore while the wind is freer offshore. So, there's little to choose between the two courses but the bigger yacht does better on the offshore course.

Wildfire was ahead of *America* when they started that leg of the course and was only 14 minutes ahead at the end of it. *America*'s logbook says that when closing the land on her inshore tack, they thought it was *Aurora* ahead of them, but it turned out to be *Wildfire* which indicates three important points:

1. *America*'s offshore tack paid off better than her crew expected.

2. Even to experts, *Wildfire* and *Aurora* looked much alike.

3. Aboard *America* they judged they were about level with *Aurora* which was a lot more likely to be correct than what our newsmen said.

The Times said *Wildfire* rounded St. Catherine's Point 3 miles ahead of *America* but someone perhaps on the Cliff timed *Wildfire* 3.45 *America* 3.59 (One and a half miles astern) and, in one version, an unidentified cutter 10 minutes astern of *America*, so this cutter was almost for certain *Aurora*. Perhaps *America*'s logbook if available might confirm or disprove this.

With a moderate breeze just before the beam *America* averaged 7.4 knots from St. Catherine's point to off Freshwater where she overhauled *Wildfire* and from there to the Needles, she averaged the same speed. *Wildfire* averaged 6.5 knots from St. Catherine's point to where *America* passed her and at that speed, she would have been two and a half minutes astern of *America* at the Needles. But *The Times* says she was 18 minutes astern. This would mean her speed had dropped from 6.5 to 4.0 knots while *America* kept on the same speed, and yet *Wildfire* finished ahead of *America*. So, all probability points to the yacht 18 minutes astern being *Aurora* since rounding St. Catherine's point she would have lost eight minutes on *America* and gained nine and a half minutes on *Wildfire* who had a stronger foul tide after

> rounding it, and probably lost a bit when she carried her balloon jib with the wind too shy for it.
>
> After *America* rounded the Needles our newsmen had far more important things to attend to than *Wildfire* or *Aurora*. There was a large fleet of spectator craft and *America* instead of taking the shortest course to the finish sailed close alongside the Royal Yacht where her crew, including the owners, in spite of being Republicans raised their hats to Queen Victoria.
>
> When the newsmen had finished making notes on all of this and had decided it was 'like the Derby favourite leaving the course after Tattenham corner' and how gratified Queen Victoria must have been, *Wildfire* had probably made a tight turn, set her balloon topsail and was well away for Cowes and lost in the crowd, so they assumed a cutter 18 minutes astern of *America* was *Wildfire* as it looked like her. It wouldn't have worried them if she was a bit more astern than they expected. But it seemed certain this that this was *Aurora*.
>
> If they thought *Aurora* was *Wildfire* and disqualified, it explains why they ignored her and how 'For an hour after *America* passed the Needles we kept the channel in view and there was no appearance of a second yacht,' and how *Aurora* could finish less than a mile astern of *America* and not be detected, and how she finished three and a quarter hours earlier than the Bell's man thought possible and why he was so certain that *Aurora*'s finishing gun must have been a mistake (fired for a disqualified yacht). None of the accepted accounts explain any of these points. There was nothing improbable about *Aurora* catching up 10 minutes on *America* in nearly three hours to the finish, it was a dead run, *America*'s weakest point of sailing and *Aurora* drew about 3 feet less water.

The running aground of the *Arrow* and the subsequent standing by of the *Alarm* were arguably further highly significant moments in the race. Two of the fastest yachts in the British fleet, perennial winners over previous seasons, they were more than the measure of the *Wildfire*.

The *Arrow*, owned by Thomas Chamberlayne at the time of the race in 1851 (previously owned by Joseph Weld), was an 84-ton cutter. It was similar in proportions to the 1848 *Wildfire*, built by Hansen of Cowes, but with a stellar pedigree in Solent races dating back to the early 1820s. The Inman of Lymington-built *Alarm*, also a potent racer, was under the ownership of

Joseph Weld for the race. The *Alarm* was considered to be one of the elite cutters at 193 tons, capable of speed-matching *America* in any kind of breeze. When the *Arrow* went aground on what are now called the Church Rocks, any realistic hope of beating *America* was effectively quashed. This was presumably on the flat sandy section on which those rocks are found closer inshore, and hence why the *Arrow* could be towed off by the excursion yacht *The Queen Her Majesty* as the *Alarm* stood by. The two best boats of the British fleet out, it was left to the *Aurora* and *Freak* to close the gap whilst the *Wildfire* was not entered and thus ineligible.

However, the race that unfolded and the narrative of the *America* being an outstanding design, superior in every way to the British fleet, is not supported by the analysis and again we turn to the historian A. E. Reynolds Brown for an explanation:

> The America Cup [sic] is the most publicised trophy of yacht racing because it is of long standing and in the first race for it, England was shamefully defeated by America, the yacht that won it – and this revolutionised yacht design as no other before or since. Much has been repeated about why she was fast this is a study to determine if by modern ideas of design research, she was fast compared to our smaller yachts or just big and lucky. America was a 90-foot schooner and in a fifty-mile race around the Isle of Wight she finished eight minutes ahead of the 57-foot cutter Aurora, so by modern rules Aurora beat her by about 30 minutes on time allowance.
>
> But the accepted story is that at the Needles only 13 miles from the finish, Aurora was out of sight between 6 and 8 miles (say 60 to 80 minutes) astern. The wind at this time was very light and America was held up by the last of the Solent ebb till the Channel ebb had brought Aurora down level with, so when the tide turned, they drifted over the finishing line almost together. A look at the tidal charts shows Aurora could not have gained more than two miles by this. The finishing times were America 8:37pm the cutters Aurora 8:45pm, Bacchante 9:30pm Eclipse 9:45pm and the Jackass Barque 'Brilliant' three and a half hours later. The cutters were much the same speed, so these times suggest a finish on a foul tide rather than a fair one.
>
> The race was sailed on a Friday and only Bell's Life in London, the sporting paper, printed a useful account next day. This said that America rounded the Needles on the last of the flood, all other competitors were

out of sight, so at least 7 miles astern and in the conditions of wind and tide none of them could finish before midnight. The breeze was lighter than it had been during the day, but Bell's gave no hint that America was becalmed before she finished. He said there was a rumour that a finishing gun for another yacht had been fired 25 minutes after America's he dismissed it as a 'mistake,' but did not make it clear what he meant; the gun had not been fired at all; or had been fired for a non-competitor like Wildfire.

The Monday papers did admit that Aurora had finished soon after America; 18 minutes after in Bell's Life, 8 minutes in The Times which is the accepted version. All had the same message. At the Needles they could not see Aurora even with their spyglasses so she must have been 6 to 8 miles astern; that after Hurst Fort the race was a 'mere drift' and should not count. So, we had suffered a humiliating defeat. Nothing about the tide, nothing about Aurora finishing three hours earlier than believed possible; in fact a pretty good cover up.

It seems it was about 30 years after the race that someone who had not read Bell's first account thought that Aurora sailing 8 to 11 miles more than America in the last three hours needed some more explanation, so he faked the time of the tide by 5 hours and our historians have repeated him ever since. High water Portsmouth was 6:24am and 7:03pm. America rounded the Needles at 5:47pm so by the Atlas of Tidal streams on the last of the FLOOD.

The distance to the finish was 13.4 miles; if she kept to the channel she would have had 6.6 miles of foul tide for a total distance through the water of 20 miles in two hours 50 minutes a speed of 7.05 knots, or if Mr Underwood, the Cowes pilot, was given a free hand (and America's log book says he did a splendid job in all her races) he might, with some tide dodging, have halved the amount of foul tide for an average speed of 5.9 knots – no great speed for a yacht of her size but an awful lot faster than a mere drift. If Aurora was 6 or 8 miles astern, she would have had a stronger foul tide after the Needles and would have averaged 7.3 to 8 knots to finish when she did. For that she would have needed a fresh breeze from the right direction the whole time which no one noticed.

So, unless someone can turn up some hard evidence against it, Aurora was no more than two and a quarter miles astern of America at the

Needles, an average of no more than 6.3 knots to the finish, but for some reason our newsmen did not see her or mistook her for some other yacht.

This analysis is highly plausible and modern tidal charts and computer simulations show that if *America* did indeed round the Needles at 5.47 pm, one hour and 16 minutes before High Water in Portsmouth, then they would have had approximately 0.7 to 0.9 knots of tide underneath them for around about half an hour to 45 minutes before the tide sluice changes direction rapidly to produce nearly 2 knots of adverse tide against them as they approached the Hurst narrows – a pinch point in the western Solent where the tide is strongest.

Even more compelling is the fact that if the *Aurora* and the *Bacchante* had hugged close inshore at Freshwater Bay, the likelihood at the time that the *America* was bearing away around the Needles, they would have been in favourable tide of between 0.2 and 0.3 knots and making good progress up behind the *America*. All accounts indicate that the wind was light all the way down the Solent, and indeed the journalists of the day mentioned that it was little of a contest for the remainder of the race.

If it was true, the alteration of course inshore to Alum Bay, where Queen Victoria was present on deck along with Prince Albert and the young Prince of Wales, is a remarkable, almost race-ruining detour. Presumably this would have been called initially by John Cox Stevens to acknowledge Her Majesty and would have had to be agreed to by Robert Underwood and Dick Brown who would have navigated inshore into foul tide and less wind – almost a suicidal racing move. It would have placed *America* almost certainly into the first of the ebb tide along the shoreline, depending on how close inshore at Alum Bay the Royal Yacht was moored. Judging by the very short time that it took Prince Albert and the Prince of Wales to go ashore and then return, we can assume that she was anchored close to the shore to take in the stunning multi-coloured sand cliffs of quartz, felspar and mica – a favourite spot for the Queen when onboard. But did this really happen? Accounts vary, but it would be a fool-hardy racing sailor that would take this option. Far more realistic would be the *Victoria & Albert* passing at some point down the Solent as Commodore Stevens recounted in his speech back in New York sometime after the race.

Doffing their caps, lowering their ensign and honouring the Queen would have been a greatly appreciated gesture and was typical of the exemplary approach that John Cox Stevens, his fellow syndicate members and the crew operated throughout the time they were in England. A gesture so well-received also set forth a train of events after the race that saw Her Majesty visit *America* to inspect the ship. The signal this sent through the court reporters in the newspapers and journals of the day stemmed, if not changed, the tide of public and political opinion of the New World, capitalising on a wave of un-ending popularity that the Queen had enjoyed since her marriage to Prince Albert.

However, a nagging positional query still stands over this race. The last recorded sighting, possibly by an onshore observer, of the *Aurora*, *Freak* and *Volante* was at Dunnose Point where it was recorded rather casually that they were 2 to 3 miles astern of *America*. In fact, analysis suggests that they were on the same tack and had actually closed the gap on *America* to some 1.4 to 2.2 miles having been to leeward by dint of the inshore course inside the Nab Light Vessel. At St. Lawrence, another observer said that *Aurora* was just one mile to leeward of *America*, which would indicate that she was catching fast and could well have been level with *America*, who was slow through the tacks, by St. Catherine's Point. This was the last record of *Aurora* before the finish and the mis-sighting of her hugging close in at Freshwater Bay, and it makes a laughing stock of records that no-one was in sight at the Needles. The finishing line win of *America* by just eight minutes indicates that *Aurora* was closing fast and the race all down the back of the Island was far closer than recounted by the newsmen of the day.

Whilst the Queen was gracious in the face of defeat, the *America*'s win in 1851 was an immediate body blow to the British who felt that their best boats had capitulated rather than posed a stern test. Henry Steers summed this up best in his Seawanhaka speech, which gave more evidence of John Cox Stevens's ability to throw the dice:

> There was an awful crying and moaning about Cowes that night we finished. Ratsey and other builders were much chagrined, but they all said that they could build a boat that could beat the America. They said that she was a mere shell, a Yankee trick, that we had exhausted ourselves. Well John C. Stevens said: 'what will you do?' They said: 'we will build a boat in 90 days that will beat the America for £500.' He said $2500 won't pay us for waiting 90 days, make it £25,000 and we'll wait and sail the race. But they would not do this and so it came to naught.

The Lawson History, however, summed up the impact in more global terms and in excellent prose commented:

> While the America's visit to England was destined to have a far reaching and important effect on British naval architecture, other influences growing out of it were of the greatest importance to the nation whose product she was. These were social and from the position of the persons concerned, in a measure political. The three men who went to England to race the America were representative Americans well suited to make a favourable impression on behalf of their people. The Stevens brothers were men of broad affairs, typical American gentleman of their time, while James A. Hamilton, son of Alexander Hamilton, was not only a gentleman and man of the world, but was active in political life, and was the friend and adviser of many of the statesman who in the first half century of the Republic shaped the destiny of the nation. Prior to their appearance in England with the America there had been very little social intercourse between the two countries, whose relations were by no means as close as they are now. The managers of the America were pioneers in international sporting events, which naturally have an important social side. Their experiences in England did more good than could be appreciated at the time.

England then openly patronised Americans and had a peculiar national idea of Yankee 'cuteness.' The experience of American travellers, and of American exhibitors at the exposition, had not been entirely pleasant, while there was a very low opinion held in England of American social life. The men who took the *America* abroad were of a stamp to command the respect of all classes of Englishmen, and they were properly greeted with cordiality, and took their places naturally among the persons of title and influence whom they met at Cowes; while the Queen signally honoured them, and without question was strongly impressed by them as men, as well as by the vessel that conveyed such an important lesson to her people. The circumstances of the visit of the *America* doubtless contributed in no small degree to the friendly feeling Victoria showed towards the American people from that time, a feeling that was in certain critical periods of more benefit to this nation than the world knew.

The timing of the Queen's visit to the *America*, set for for 4pm but later recorded by Her Majesty in her journals as being at some time after 5.30pm, the day after the race on the 23 August, could be argued to have influenced somewhat the breathless and extended copy of the subsequent article that appeared in The Times on the 25 August, the Monday after the race when the reporter would have had time to digest the information that had been made available to him.

Queen Victoria's attitude towards the *America* and the gentlemen of the New York Yacht Club, whom as we see above, she so admired 'as men', would have undoubtedly set the tone for the court reporters and would have reflected in the underlying narrative of relative invincibility that they wrote. Her visit to the boat was a mere half an hour, accompanied by Prince Albert and a further party of court gentlemen plus two ladies-in-waiting, Lady Desart and Miss Bing. The visit had been arranged by the Marquess of Anglesey's son, Lord Alfred Paget, one of the Queen's attendants and was marked by formality with the Queen inspecting the quarter-deck with Commodore Stevens, exchanging pleasantries, before requesting to look below deck.

In a flash it was over, but the signal that it sent of acceptance was immense. Queen Victoria had been genuinely impressed by the performance of the *America* in the RYS £100 Cup race and the conduct of the crew in approaching her, wherever in the Solent that may have been, and saluting – a rare thing for a Republican nation to accede to. The honour of dipping the national ensign as Queen Victoria arrived and left the *America,* it was reported, was duly followed impeccably on her visit – repeating the gesture recorded on the fly-past on their way to victory and history.

Queen Victoria, writing in her journal at the end of the day on 23 August 1851, recorded her visit to the *America,* clearly showing a genuine interest in its design:

> A dull and showery morning. After breakfast walking, writing & painting with Mr. Leitch. In the afternoon, playing & singing. At half past five, we drove down with the Ladies & Gentlemen to the pier, where we got into the barge, and went on board the 'America', which had been brought round on purpose for us to see her. She is extremely pretty, from her great simplicity. Hardly any rigging, and the sails strapped down to the boom; wide in the centre, & gradually tapering, into a sharp point. She is very low in the water and there is a bulwark of only a foot high. In the stern is a round well with seats round it, 'according to the fashion of our country' as the owner said. There is a great deal of accommodation below, and the decorations and fittings are very pretty. When we left and had landed, we had 2 hauls from the beach but caught no fish. — No addition to our dinner party. We sang after dinner.

Writing some years later, in 1893, the great yacht designer Lewis Herreshoff summed up the impact of the visit of *America* to British shores, saying:

> The racing of the 'America' in England 42 years ago has without doubt had more influence, directly and indirectly, on the yachting world than the performance of any other yacht, and both countries concerned owe to her designer and owners a debt of gratitude that will remain uncancelled for generations; for it has been the means of bringing the two yachting nations together in many friendly contests, resulting not only in marked modifications in the form and rig of the yachts of both countries, but the social intercourse begun so many years ago has continued and increased greatly to the benefit of yachting, and has led to a more complete union of all interested in the promotion of close international relations.

In truth, the crew of *America* both charmed and bluffed (through outlandish sums of money wagered but not taken) that summer. It was a remarkable sporting achievement to take on the best of the British fleet and win on home waters – something that no British boat has been able to repeat to this day in trying to regain the America's Cup. History records excellence, whilst common sense and analysis sees it differently, but the legend of the Cup was crafted in 1851 and the start of the longest winning sporting streak in history was about to begin.

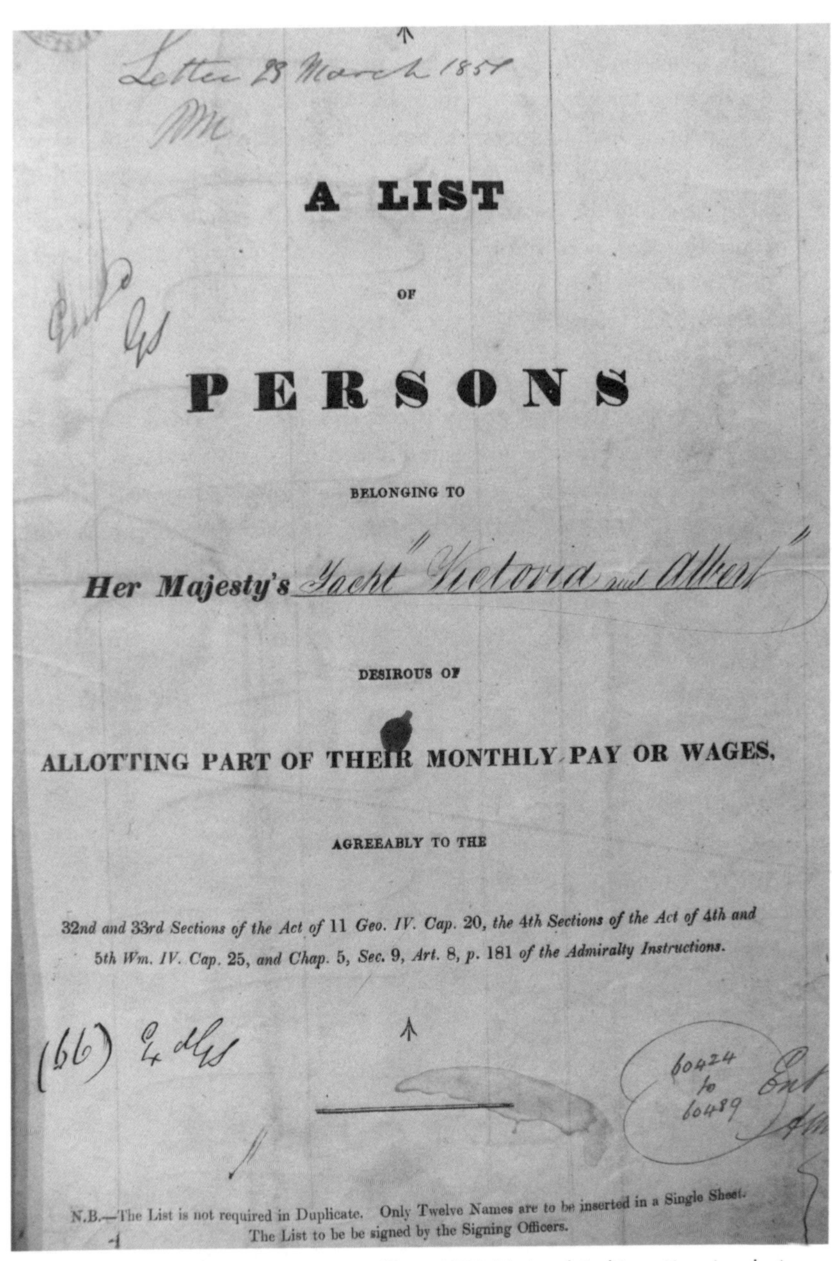

Letter 28 March 1851

A LIST

OF

PERSONS

BELONGING TO

Her Majesty's Yacht "Victoria and Albert"

DESIROUS OF

ALLOTTING PART OF THEIR MONTHLY PAY OR WAGES,

AGREEABLY TO THE

32nd and 33rd Sections of the Act of 11 *Geo. IV. Cap.* 20, *the* 4*th Sections of the Act of* 4*th and* 5*th Wm. IV. Cap.* 25, *and Chap.* 5, *Sec.* 9, *Art.* 8, *p.* 181 *of the Admiralty Instructions.*

(66)

60424 to 60489

N.B.—The List is not required in Duplicate. Only Twelve Names are to be inserted in a Single Sheet. The List to be be signed by the Signing Officers.

The wage docket for the HMY *Victoria & Albert*, 1851 (National Archives, Kew, London).

CHAPTER SEVEN

CHASING THE CUP'S 'APOCRYPHAL' GRAIL – THE 'SIGNAL-MASTER'

Truth is never to be expected from authors whose understanding is warped with enthusiasm.
John Dryden

The genesis of this book was a desire to solve a mystery, a legend if you will, of the America's Cup. Over nine months it became an absorbing, often fruitless, desperate search through a myriad of agencies, record keepers, libraries, documents and reference books. The doors of which, as is so often in the case of British yachting, its clubs and naval circles, have been found to be somewhat diffident, antipathetic and mistrusting to prise open. But the curiosity never ended and the persistence to succeed simply got stronger with every blind alley. Even to the last second, with the facts unknowingly within reach, hopes were seemingly dashed and another dead-end felt all too familiar.

The great serial America's Cup winner Grant Dalton, CEO of the mighty Emirates Team New Zealand and defender of the 37th America's Cup in Barcelona in 2024, stated it so compellingly in the video in the America's Cup Experience exhibition in Barcelona which I helped to curate: 'The best quote in the America's Cup is "There is no second" – if you win, you take the Cup, if you don't, you have nothing. Nobody enters the America's Cup to not try and win it, it's too expensive and it's too difficult.'

However, attribution of this famous quote, as uttered to Queen Victoria, has seemingly been lost in time and history, with many leading journalists and historians writing it off as an 'apocryphal' tale and looking no further. Easy to discount, it has been much harder to prove. Even the *Lawson History* has a wonderful line that says 'History does not preserve the name of this perspicacious sea-dog', and it was this that drove me to write this book and do the research. Who was the mystery signal-master on the deck of the *Victoria & Albert?*

The America's Cup is unique in that there is no overarching governing body as in soccer with FIFA and UEFA, the Olympic Games, Formula 1 or Tennis. It's totally unique. If you win, you win it all. You name the boats, the venue, the rules, the dates and, as we will see in subsequent chapters, the rules are arcanely squared towards the Defending yacht club and its syndicate.

Happily, the America's Cup exists with this imparity and over the years some of the world's most swashbuckling and intriguing millionaires and billionaires have teamed up with some of the greatest, most innovative companies and talented sailors in a most-likely futile attempt to win. The odds against winning are simply enormous. Nearly all the teams start at a design disadvantage and it's a game of trying to leapfrog, predict and capitalise on research that makes the difference. This is why in the modern America's Cup we see the rise of artificial intelligence to create literally millions of simulations for everything from hull shape down to individual componentry. It's the elixir aligned with the impossible dream, as well as both national and personal pride, that keeps the wealthy coming.

The unique structure of the America's Cup was ultimately the result of the original Deed of Gift, which I will come onto in the next chapter. However, the conversation that encapsulated the event in 1851, and does so today, was allegedly held onboard Her Majesty's Yacht, the *Victoria & Albert,* on the afternoon of the 22 August 1851, between Queen Victoria and her 'signal-master', whose name had seemingly been lost in the annals of history.

> 'Say Signal-Master, are the yachts in sight?' The Queen asked,
>
> 'Yes, may it please Your Majesty.' Replied the Signal-Master.
>
> 'Which is first?'
>
> 'The America.'
>
> 'And who is second?'
>
> 'Ah Your Majesty, there is no second.'

How this conversation could possibly have been recorded is, and shall remain, a mystery. If it did indeed take place at all, the wording would have to have been manually recorded and noted once ashore, then relayed to, possibly, a Cowes reporter sometime after the event, perhaps even the next day. No reporters were allowed onboard the Royal Yacht and indeed it is known that *The Times* reporter was stationed onboard a steamship which followed the race in 1851 and may well have relied on 'spotters' dotted around the Isle of Wight at key points to narrate the race afterwards. Obviously, no telecommunications were in place in 1851, so the natural conclusion is that some of the reported positionings and observations relied on annotation relayed at a later time and date with the unfortunate consequence of miscommunication or skewed communication to fit the overall narrative of the final report.

One of the most curious pieces of the overall report (published in full in Chapter 5 of this book) was the almost certainly 'apocryphal' line 'Off Cowes were innumerable yachts and on every side was heard the hail: "Is the America first?" – the answer "Yes." "What's second?" – the reply "Nothing."'

Again, how could a reporter following the race onboard a steamship know this, especially amongst a cacophony of boats that had gathered for the end of the Royal Yacht Squadron's regatta, eagerly awaiting the evening's fireworks and perhaps interested only in the race itself as a side-show. The historian A. E. Reynolds Brown makes the assertion that the *Wildfire* actually beat *America* across the finish line, although not officially recorded in the results owing to its Irish owners not actually entering the race and the yacht's shifting sand-ballasted design not being favoured by the Royal Yacht Squadron. So again, the chances of local sailors claiming 'nothing' was behind or ahead of the *America* is likely journalist licence feeding into the invincibility narrative – a common journalistic trait during the period.

What we do know, due to naval records and also confirmed in *The Times* article of the 25 August 1851, is that the Royal Yacht *Victoria & Albert* was accompanied up the Solent by Her Majesty's yacht *Fairy*, a 312-ton, screw-driven, iron support vessel, built in 1845 by the Ditchburn & Mare yard of shipwright Thomas J. Ditchburn and the naval architect Charles John Mare in London. She was commanded by Master David Nairne Welch of Portsmouth and was officially recognised as a 'tender' to the paddle-driven Royal Yacht *Victoria & Albert* commanded by Lord Adolphus Fitzclarence R. N., the seventh natural child of King William IV and Mrs Dorothy Jordan, a famous actress who bore the King ten children before he married Princess Adelaide of Saxe-Meiningen in 1818.

The *Victoria & Albert* weighed anchor in Alum Bay, a popular and quite wind-sheltered bay which lies out of the very fast running tide of the main channel, immediately to the right of the outcrop of white rocks that forms the famous Needles waypoint when looking easterly down the Solent. Racing sailors today avoid getting sucked into Alum Bay where the winds are fickle, and for the *America*, who rounded the Needles at 5.47 pm, some 1 hour and 16 minutes before the High-Water time at Portsmouth of 7.03 pm, the tide would have been adverse inshore according to modern tide tables. It is highly likely that the *Victoria & Albert* would have been set at anchor to the very first of the ebb tide at the time of the *America*'s rounding with her port side being the optimal viewing side as the yacht passed by.

Ahead of the rounding of *America*, it is recorded that both the *Victoria & Albert* and the HMY *Fairy* had ventured out beyond the Needles at 4.20 pm, presumably to try and sight the yachts. The *Victoria & Albert* returned and by 4.40 pm had dropped anchor in Alum Bay. The *Fairy*, in company, was then sent as a spotter ship to relay, by signal, the positioning of the yachts as the race came into view. We know that the Royal Yacht was briefly at anchor in Alum Bay, as was reported by *The Times* (25 August 1851), although it was certainly enough time for Prince Albert and the Prince of Wales to be taken ashore by a rowing team in the ship's scull tenders.

The HMY *Fairy* would have stood out beyond the Needles, but in order to relay a signal back to the *Victoria & Albert*, it would almost certainly have headed westwards but quite how far is not recorded. The curiosity of the Isle of Wight at that point is that it is incredibly difficult to see beyond what is now known as St. Anthony Rock. This feature juts out quite markedly in 'Sun Corner' just around the outcrop of rocks that form the Needles and precludes any kind of decent view of Freshwater Bay where the smaller cutters *Wildfire* and *Aurora* would almost certainly have been plying their way in the least adverse tide, running at approximately 0.3 to 0.2 knots at two hours before High Water Portsmouth. This is perhaps one of the most crucial details of the race and indeed the story of the America's Cup, but naval records do not record the precise location of the HMY *Fairy* when she would have hand-signalled with flags back to the *Victoria & Albert*. However, we can say with absolute certainty that a line of sight would have needed to be maintained between the two vessels, and in that case, a dead reckoning would put the HMY *Fairy* to the west of the Needles point, in the main fairway channel, but not too far out, for good seamanship.

As the *America*, who had taken a more southerly route along the back of the Isle of Wight than the tide-cheating and much smaller cutters inshore, came into view, the hurried signal would have been made back to the

Victoria & Albert by the *Fairy*'s signal-master. With only fairly rudimentary telescopes, and almost half a century before Guglielmo Marconi invented a ship-worthy communications system, the flags would have been received by the Yeoman of the Signals onboard the *Victoria & Albert*, before the message was relayed to Her Majesty Queen Victoria and the rest of the Royal party.

The search for the name of the 'signal-master' encompassed the Royal Archives and the Royal Naval Archives with cross referencing between the two over a number of months before eventually reaching the National Archives in Kew, London, on the back of a dearth of recorded information from the day in 1851.

What was unavailable, and not of record, was a crew list from onboard the Royal Yacht, which required some lateral thinking from the archivist at the Royal Archives, Julie Crocker, who wrote in August 2023:

> While we do have some papers here relating to HMY Victoria and Albert, I'm afraid we do not have any lists of the crew. We have always believed such information to be held in the Admiralty papers at The National Archives, but it sounds as if you have already looked there without any success. I have looked in the printed Royal Kalendar (sic) for 1851 which has some information about the Royal Navy, but under HMY Victoria and Albert it only lists the Captain (Lord Adolphus Fitzclarence) and the Commander (W. Crispin).

However, what Ms Crocker did suggest was filing a search query with the National Archives and Records Administration (NARA) whose Remote Enquiries Duty Officer, James Cronan, came back with an intriguing email in September 2023 stating:

> The Royal Yacht 'Victoria & Albert' (1843) was operated by the Royal Navy and as such there are no crew lists but instead there is a ships muster. The muster for 'Victoria and Albert' for the period 1851–1853 is held under catalogue reference ADM 38/9254. There are also registers of allotments recording wages of crew which were sent back to their families. Registers of allotments for 'Victoria and Albert' for 1851 are held in ADM 27/113. There are also ships logs. The ships log for 'Victoria and Albert' covering 1 January to 7 September 1851 is held in ADM 53/4308.
>
> These documents have not been digitised. You or somebody acting on your behalf, are welcome to visit us to look at the original records.

This felt like a breakthrough in the search for the 'signal-master' and with huge anticipation, a visit was arranged to the National Archives' quite phenomenal facility at Kew, not far from the River Thames in south-west London. It's a highly secure facility but accessible to all following the requisite registration, photo evidence, account set-up and screening. Historians, students, and the curious fill the hushed halls of this thermo-controlled environment with vast tabling arrangements replete with viewing lamps and desktop magnifying glasses once through the guarded entrance with its magnetic ESA antenna barriers preventing any unlawful removal of documentation.

Having already requested in advance the three documents that I wished to view, the attendants had them prepared in order within a secure wooden cabinet but could only be viewed one at a time and had to be signed for and returned before the next could be viewed. Issued with white gloves, the attendant took out the first 'box' containing the muster under the code ADM 38/9254 and instructed that none of the documents that I had requested had been opened, 'perhaps since being originally archived in the 1850s', and that the use of polystyrene book supports would be necessary to support the spines. Kindly, the lady showed me how to view these historic records and I was set up on a table with a powerful lamp. To be honest, the feeling was like touching the Holy Grail of our sport, real history was before me, and the crumbling, dry-aged smell of the books was something that hit the senses immediately – these records had never been opened in perhaps 172 years.

The chronicling was detailed but, in many cases, unreadable, handwritten in rather beautiful and lavish script and at huge length. Each document had a minimum of 400 pages and starting from the back, as instructed by the attendant to protect the integrity of the spine, I gingerly began turning the pages to find the relevant dates. What started out with hope quickly became despair as the records around the 22 August 1851 were either missing or irrelevant. The first recorded activity on the day stated 'Cleaning ships. Bridge cleaning completed. Room and Paintwork. Lit the fires. Coals aboard 55 tons.'

The record then went on to state:

> 11.50 Came to Thorley. 2.25 left for Osborne. 3.15 Proceeded full speed with Her Majesty onboard. 5.00 Stopped before Needles. 7.40 stopped off Osborne. 7.55 Proceeded. 8.15 Came to the jetty off Cowes. Blew the fires and blew the water out of the boilers.

This official account and the ship's log rather questions *The Times* reporting of 25 August 1851 (reproduced in full pp86–87) that:

> Two of the excursion steamers ran into Alum Bay and anchored there to see the race round the Needles. While waiting there in intense anxiety for the first vessel that should shoot round the immense pillars of chalk and limestone which bear the name, the passengers were delighted to behold the *Victoria and Albert* with the Royal standard at the main and the Lord Admiral's flag at the fore, steaming round from northwest followed by the *Fairy* and the little dockyard tender. Her Majesty, the Prince and the Royal family, were visible by the aid of a glass from the deck of the steamers. The Royal yacht went past the Needles accompanied by the *Fairy* at 5:35, but quickly returned, and at 5:45 lay off Alum Bay. The *Fairy* was signalled to proceed around the Needles to bring tidings of the race and at once posted Ariel-like on her errand.

The Times account contradicts the official document at the National Archives that the Royal Yacht passed the Needles at 4.20 pm and was at Alum Bay by 4.40 pm as the timings simply do not work. *The Times* correspondent once again may have used some journalistic licence to create the story as the naval timeline shows that the *Victoria & Albert* was in Alum Bay over an hour before the *America* rounded, which would have given Prince Albert and the Prince of Wales enough time to go briefly ashore as documented in the article.

What the record does not show is the weigh anchor time of the Royal Yacht and whether she remained at station until the *America* passed. This has been suggested in numerous historic narratives along with the account that the *Victoria & Albert* passed the *America* for a second time at some point down the Solent, where again pleasantries were conveyed before the Royal Party made their way down to anchor off East Cowes for transfer back to the royal residence at Osborne House.

Returning this first document to the attendant, having duly packaged it correctly and sealed it as instructed, the next was delivered to my table. This contained detailed accounts of the movement of the *Elfin* – a small paddle steamer, which was used to transport the Queen and her attendants from the East Cowes landing jetty out to the Royal Yacht. The *Elfin* was first commissioned in 1849 specifically for the purpose of ferrying the royal party and also for obtaining supplies from Southampton and Portsmouth for the Queen when in residence on the Isle of Wight. By all accounts it was lavishly decorated in the style of the day across two decks and its plans are held at the Royal Museums in Greenwich. It stayed in service until the Queen's death in 1901.

The second document had little to add to the story of the race on 22 August but does give an account of the visit to the *America* the day after the race: '11.40 Elfin arrives at Cowes. 1.45 Elfin left Osborne. 4.50 Shackled on to Osbourne Priory. 4.55 Elfin left for Cowes. 5.45 The Queen went aboard the America Schooner Yacht. 6.10 The Queen alighted from the America.'

Again, this was useful detail regarding the timeline, but the real crux of information, the spine-tingling moment, came in the third document of the series suggested by the National Archives ADM 53/4308. This was delivered to the table with a string seal which was wired around the wooden box and as the archivist began to untangle it, the rope disintegrated completely, indicating that this had not been touched by human hands since its original archiving. Strange to think that in the storied history of the America's Cup, and the number of writers and historians who have covered this fascinating event, that no-one in recent times had thought to tap the resources of the National Archives. But here it was, a detailed account of payments made by the Admiralty to the ship's companies of every vessel operating under the auspices of the Royal Navy in the period covering 1851. However, history wasn't to be kind and the 'apocryphal' name of the 'signal-master' that could possibly have uttered the words 'Ah Your Majesty. There is no second' wasn't easy to find.

The document was huge, 500 pages and, once placed on the polystyrene support and the back cover opened, its spine immediately disintegrated leaving shards of brown paper and rudimentary string binding amidst hardened glue on the table below and a sigh from the attendant: 'This happens quite often with documents of this era,' she said. And it got worse, as the pages were turned, many became loose leafed and the paper quality itself was brittle requiring the most delicate of touches. As I scanned each page, every conceivable ship that was operating at the time was recorded, some in exquisite detail, others with the briefest of mentions often detailing only a skeleton of staff of maybe two or three on its vast pages. Her Majesty's ships included the *Dauntless, Leander, Excellent, Growler, Albion, Daedalus, Blenheim, Penelope, Resistance, Britannia, Superb, Trafalgar, Victory* and the *St. George* – all documented exquisitely with wage packets and addresses where stipends would be sent by the ratings and officers of Her Majesty's fleet.

A quarter of the way in, I found an entry for the HMY *Victoria & Albert*, and it was one of extreme brevity detailing payments made to Lord Adolphous Fitzclarence, the captain and William Crispin,[1] the ship's commander. At that point in the journey to find the 'signal-master' it very much felt like it was all over. The journey to the National Archives had been a wasted trip but for some reason I kept turning the pages from back to front passing hugely detailed accounts of larger ships' companies with everything from landing officers to ship's maids, officers of all rank and deckhands listed endlessly. Page after page was turned as the beginning of the book neared ever closer before one remarkably beautifully written section just pages before the end, the beginning in fact, elicited the thought 'wouldn't it be amazing if this was the *Victoria & Albert?*'

With some trepidation, I turned the pages to find that, in fact, it was. Here, finally, was a full crew list plus details of each member's rank and indeed the address and names to which their monthly wage was paid, as was the trend at the time. The search for the 'signal-master' was suddenly very real. History was being kind at long last.

What the document showed most clearly was that the *Victoria & Albert* had in her employ two 'Yeoman of Signals' – John Mellin and Henry Wickham – two names that have never before been associated with the America's Cup and the story of the first race around the Isle of Wight in 1851. Mellin's address is listed as 'Portsea, Hants' (Hampshire) whilst Wickham is listed as living in Bath, Somerset. Both Mellin and Wickham had relatives who were residents of 'Landport', the area of Portsea Island where Portsmouth expanded in the 19th century and which took its name from the Landport Gate. The wage dockets show that John Mellin sent a monthly stipend to his mother, Charlotte Mellin, whilst Wickham assigned his wage packet to his sister, Martha Wickham.

John Mellin (Royal Navy Service Number: 294834) was almost certainly the senior Yeoman of Signals onboard the *Victoria & Albert* as he was aged 30 when he entered service on the ship. He was promoted on the 21 December 1851 to what the journal entry describes as 'Captain of Cox's' – almost certainly a coxswain role commanding the Queen's barge, perhaps *Elfin*

[1] I discovered that Crispin had married Caroline Busfeild Ferrand in 1845, but tragically she died the following year giving birth to twin daughters and is buried in the old cemetery in West Lulworth in a grave surrounded by iron railings. The daughters were named Victoria and Albertine and their baptism was sponsored by Queen Victoria and Prince Albert. Crispin went on to command the HMY *Fairy* from 1853 to 1855.

although there is no record of this available. Mellin served the Royal Yacht through to discharge on the 10 February 1853. Henry Wickham (Royal Navy Service Number: 284849) was 26 when he entered service on the *Victoria & Albert* and served through to the 17 July 1852.

As a team, Mellin and Wickham would have operated from the outside bridge of the *Victoria & Albert* and would have watched the movements of HMY *Fairy* using telescopes. Once under signalling, it would be the senior Yeoman of the Signals calling the flag communication whilst the junior deciphered. It was unlikely that either flag or light semaphore was used as the adoption of flag semaphore was still some way away in 1866. Light semaphore – the deciphering of dots and dashes from a signal lamp – was first adopted by Captain, later Vice-Admiral, Philip Howard Colomb in 1867.

The communication system most likely used by Mellin and Wickham would have been according to the *Admiralty Book of Signals*, published in January 1851 and adopted across all naval vessels for that year before being updated. It is almost certain that the Yeoman of Signals of each yacht would have agreed before dock-out on a specific set of signals to record the *America*, and likely a code sheet for the rest of the fleet, although naval records do not record this, nor the signals made back to the Royal yacht.

The signalling back to Mellin and Wickham would thus have been short and concise. With all likelihood that the *Fairy* would have been unable to sight the *Wildfire* and the *Aurora* in Freshwater Bay, the signal that would have been taken was, on the face of it, no more than a record of the facts that the Yeoman of Signals could see or would have been informed about and relayed back to the *Victoria & Albert*. The interpretation of that signal and the subsequent telling of it to an enquiring Queen, seated presumably on the aft deck in anticipation of seeing the winner round the Needles and enter the Solent, is perhaps a happy accident of inference, rather than a pointed analysis or synopsis of the race itself. 'Perspicacious', therefore, is almost certainly a comment in hindsight, written many years after the race in reflection of what it would become and what it is today.

Whilst the signalling would have been directed at the *Victoria & Albert*, several other steamships in the area, and almost certainly the one carrying *The Times* reporter, would have decoded the message from HMY *Fairy*. But with no means of getting that message down as far as Cowes – a good 13 miles away – the story in *The Times* of 'innumerable yachts and on every side was heard the hail: "Is the America first?" – the answer "Yes." "What's second?" – the reply "Nothing,"' is most likely the most 'apocryphal' story of them all.

What is curious, however, is the route of the *America* to pass the *Victoria & Albert*. With over an hour of flood tide running from west to east and the beginning of the ebb inshore at Alum Bay, it was almost a kamikaze act of navigation by Robert Underwood to bring the under-canvassed, and downwind deficient schooner so close in under the cliffs. This almost certainly did not happen. The *America* would have to have passed the Needles in the safety of the main channel with easily 0.9–1.1 knots of tide underneath her keel. But to then turn quite hard to starboard in the lee of the chalk rocks of the Needles point and then run/reach into the high sandstone-covered Alum Bay with a dying south-south-westerly breeze is almost unfathomable to a racing sailor trying to win a race with fast cutters coming up from behind. There is still a significant, and very difficult, tidal stretch of water to cover to Cowes. Several accounts report that *America* ran 'slowly past the *Victoria & Albert*' as the crew doffed their caps and lowered their ensign as a sign of respect. Again, this is very unlikely to have happened in Alum Bay.

Colonel Hamilton, who sailed onboard the *America*, recounted this affair somewhat differently at a speech back in New York after the race and the dots are somewhat joined:

> After passing the Needles, we were overtaken by the royal steam yacht Victoria & Albert, with Her Majesty and her family on board, who had come down to witness the trial of speed between the models adopted by the old world and those of the new. As the steamer slowly passed us, we had the gratification of tendering our homage to the Queen after the fashion of her own people, by taking off our hats and dipping our flags. At this time, the wind had fallen to a light breeze, and we did not arrive at the flag-ship until dark. I could not learn correctly at what time or in what order the others arrived.

The Hamilton recount is more likely to be accurate as to the course into Alum Bay, and the subsequent passing of a waving Queen, so often depicted in paintings and recounted without thought or knowledge of the area, simply does not make sense to anyone who has sailed in those waters. It is highly likely that Captain Fitzclarence would have weighed anchor on the *Victoria & Albert* almost immediately upon receiving the signal that the *America* was in sight and would have sailed due north or north east to deeper water in order to make use of the main fairway channel with its favourable tide at that time. Passing the *America* in the area before the Hurst Channel pinch point of the Solent, or immediately after, as is also depicted in paintings, is a plausible explanation. Following on from this, the *Victoria & Albert* would have steamed on to Cowes to offboard the Royal party at East Cowes, arriving at Osborne as the records show at 7.40 pm, well ahead of the *America* which finished the race between a marker boat and Cowes Castle.

That it took almost three hours to cover the distance from the Needles to Cowes shows the adverse ebb tide, which the *America* would have faced on the way down the Solent, building all the way and running at approximately 3 to 3.9 knots at various waypoints down the Solent. Little surprise, therefore, that on its weakest point of sailing, goose-winging to try and make the best of the breeze, the *America* was caught so dramatically by the *Aurora*, who the Royal Yacht Squadron records show finishing at 8.45 pm (railway time) just eight minutes behind *America*.[2] It is interesting to note that nothing was said of the fast-catching *Aurora* by any of the American crew following the race, and the very fact that the name *Aurora* is not engraved on the America's Cup trophy alongside some 13 other listed finishers is an aberration lost in time. However, this embellishes the words most likely uttered by John Mellin, Yeoman of Signals, to Queen Victoria that 'There is no second.'

Whatever the truth of the mystery surrounding the quotation, and indeed several facets of the race as recorded in history and repeated in countless tomes on the America's Cup, reporting at the time was a mixture of both pleasing the editor of the newspaper and further of reader-delighting with a mix of royalty and sporting excellence, mixed with an undercurrent of establishment dissent, that played most squarely into a narrative that very much suited the Americans.

Even the finishing time of *Aurora* is a source of debate with many sources quoting that she was up to 16 minutes astern at the finish. The very fact that Colonel Hamilton couldn't distinguish who was behind, or indeed ahead, if the *Wildfire* really did finish in front, added to the confusion that surrounded Cowes that evening. The harbour entrance, known colloquially as 'Cowes Roads', was filled with boats eager to see that marvel of the Victorian era, the

[2] Railway time was the standardisation of time across the railway network – using Greenwich Mean Time – first instigated by the Great Western Railway in England in November 1840.

planned fireworks display that marked the end of the Royal Yacht Squadron Regatta of 1851.

The crowds along the front that evening were also there to see the magnificence of the fireworks crowding the gas-lamp filled promenade, and it could quite easily be argued therefore that the race finish was a sideshow of interest. The band playing 'Yankee Doodle Dandy' as *America* crossed the finish line was almost certainly a journalist construct that fitted the overall narrative. But it was, nonetheless, in the annals of some historic tomes such as *The Lawson History*, a quaint and nuanced way of clawing back some national pride from the disaster that was the American representation at the Great Exhibition.

Whatever the true facts, one thing is certain. In the race itself, the *America* won. Following a protest lodged after racing by George Ackers, owner of the schooner *Brilliant*, subsequently withdrawn after consultation with senior members of the Royal Yacht Squadron, *America*'s victory in the race was confirmed, and the 'RYS £100 Cup' – often misnamed subsequently as a 'Queen's Cup' (which it wasn't) – was awarded to Commodore Stevens.

The legend that built around the design, however, should be seen for what it was – *America* was not a rocket-ship, although she was a fast boat in 'pilot' conditions of straight-line sailing to windward and whilst power-reaching with the wind on the beam. She was desperately slow in the tacks, taking anything up to five minutes to get through the wind and, being so under-canvassed, extremely sluggish downwind. The yacht's future racing pedigree more than bears out these observations.

New York ~~May 15 1852~~ July 8 - 1857.

To the Secretary of the
New York Yacht Club.

Sir,

The undersigned, members of the New York Yacht Club, & late owners of the Schooner Yacht America, beg leave through you to present to the Club, the Cup won by the America at the Regatta of the Royal Yacht Squadron at Cowes England August 22d 1851.

This cup was offered as a prize to be sailed for by Yachts of all nations, without regard to difference of tonnage, going round the Isle of Wight (the usual course for the annual regatta of the Royal Yacht Squadron) & was won by the America, beating eight cutter & seven schooner Yachts which started in the race.

The Cup is offered to the New York Yacht Club, subject to the following conditions—

Any organised Yacht Club of any foreign ~~nation~~ country shall always be entitled through any one or more of its members to claim the right of sailing a match for this Cup with any Yacht or other vessel of not less than thirty or more than three hundred tons, measured by the Custom house rule of the Country to which the vessel belongs.

The parties desiring to sail for the Cup, may make any match with the Yacht Club in possession of the same that may be determined upon by mutual

The original Deed of Gift written by George L. Shuyler and presented to the New York Yacht Club in July 1857.

CHAPTER EIGHT

LIFE AFTER THE CUP

Like Jupiter among the Gods, America is first, and there is no second.
US Congressman Daniel Webster

Alongside the request by Her Majesty Queen Victoria to visit the *America* on the evening of 23 August 1851, the day after her victory in the race around the Isle of Wight, the gentlemen of the Royal Yacht Squadron extended every courtesy possible to the victorious owners and crew. At a senior level in the club, it had a galvanising effect with Lord Wilton leading the charm offensive and extending membership of the prestigious club to Commodore Stevens and Colonel Hamilton, who later described the conviviality and respect that they were treated to in his memoirs: 'We were elected honorary members of the club, invited to the houses of several of its members, and treated in the handsomest manner by the gentlemen of the club.'

Two days after the visit, and in deference to it, the *America* was rather expected to compete for the Queen's Cup, a trophy donated by Her Majesty to the Royal Yacht Squadron but with a summer morning lending only a sub-6 knot breeze, the decision was taken by Commodore Stevens not to start. However, as the breeze filled an hour and a half later, the crew decided to follow the fleet down towards the Nab light vessel and beat back up to Cowes. She finished second having eclipsed the likes of the *Brilliant*, the *Alarm* and the *Volante*, leaving Squadron members in no doubt that she would have won the race, had she started with the fleet. Commodore Stevens's obsession that the *America* should not start in under 6 knots of breeze, for any challenge that summer, perhaps another gambler's bluff, looked rather exposed on the 25 August 1851.

However, the concluding race that summer was against an old friend Robert Stephenson MP, who Commodore Stevens knew well through his involvement with the railways. It was very much a gentleman's sporting gesture pitting the 100-ton iron-clad *Titania* against *America*. The trial of speed very nearly didn't happen with dates clashing and then subsequent repairs to *America* who had lost part of her keel shoe the day before the race was scheduled on the 28 August 1851.

Once again, the gentlemen of the Royal Yacht Squadron, working in conjunction with the Admiral at Portsmouth, swung into action on behalf of their American friends and secured a dry-dock to affect the repair. Whilst in dock, for only eight hours, the admiralty took measurements of the yacht, and it was reported that crowds flocked to see the vessel out of the water, such was the curiosity that had built around it that summer. She was re-floated at 8 pm and docked-out to return to Cowes ahead of the race with a sum of money, £500 quoted in some cases, $500 in other recants, lodged with Lord Wilton on the outcome.

A detailed account of the race against the *Titania* was written by an observer following on a steamship, some of which is pertinent to the after-life of the *America*:

> The course appointed for this trial was, that they should proceed outside the island to a distance of twenty miles south-east of the Nab Light, where a station vessel was to be placed, and the yachts having rounded the same, were to make their way back to the Nab Light. Thus, two points of sailing would be decided – outwards with the wind large, and a dead beat homewards. The day opened with every appearance of a strong wind for the contest, and in the morning the yachts left Cowes for the rendezvous off the Nab, bearing W.S.W. from them, the Queen steamer, Captain D. Corke, having been expressly engaged to proceed out as the station vessel. At 9 o'clock the steamer left Cowes, having John Bates, Esq., the Squadron's secretary on board, and proceeded to the appointed place. The wind was strong from N.N.W. throughout the forenoon, and in the afternoon a fresh gale prevailed. A more fitting opportunity or better day could not have happened for so interesting a trial.

The fresh gale would certainly have been favourable to the *America*: these were the kinds of conditions that she excelled in as a pilot boat design, which could put out to sea in any weather to guide the Atlantic steamships into harbour. These were the kinds of conditions that George Steers had designed the boat for in British waters and were very much what John Cox Stevens and the syndicate owners had expected. As the race progressed, the *America*'s advantage became clear:

> At 1h. 30m. the hull of the America was 'fast rising,' but the Titania's hull was invisible; in five minutes afterwards, she was seen to gybe, but seemed to be 'steering wild,' the America being well handled, both being under a cloud of canvass, each having square sails, the Titania with topsail, but the America no gaff-top-sail, but apparently a water-sail, which was now taken in.
>
> At 1h. 53m. Titania lowered her square topsail, and at 1h. 56m. the America hauled down her square-sail and prepared to round the steamer. The manner in which she came on, 'as easy as a Limerick glove,' was admired by all on board. The following is the order and time of rounding the steamer: 2 hours, 3 minutes (America) to 2 hours 8 minutes and 2 seconds (Titania).
>
> Thus, there was difference of 5 minutes and 2 seconds in favour of the Yankee. As the America rounded, they stated that they had carried away the jaws of their main-gaff, but that they had secured it. Both yachts, after rounding the steamer, luffed up on the port tack, and reached in to the eastward of the Owers. There was now a fresh gale from the northward, and the steamer's head was turned in shore, the wind 'dead on end,' and plenty of it to test the relative merits of these vessels, the America being perfectly upright, and 'slipping gracefully through it.' On the contrary, the Titania 'bowed,' or rather 'dipped her nose into it.'

The reduced sail plan of the *America* was the key here and despite efforts by the crew of *Titania* to wet her sails and make them more rigid, they were eventually forced to reef the mainsail. More perfect conditions for the *America* to show her outright speed in a straight-line could not be wished for.

> We watched their progress minutely. The Titania wetted her sails, but all efforts even to recover her former position, appeared useless. The distance between the two yachts increased and became visibly 'more and more' as they progressed inshore.

At 3h. 30m. they tacked to the westward. The Culver Cliff bore N.W.½N. from the steamer; the America from the latter E.N.E., and the Titania S.E. by E. At 3h 30m. the yachts had a strong wind to contend with, and both worked towards the Nab with the ebb in their favour. A better day – wind or tide – could not have been appointed.

The Titania was then observed with her topmast struck and under her three jibs, foresail and mainsail, the America with main sail, foresail, and fore-staysail, all without a reef in, and as 'upright as a top.' At 4h. 8m. Culvers, bearing N. W, ½W. America S.E., Titania S.E. by S., and four miles dead to leeward of her antagonist. The America tacked to the northward, Titania keeping her reach to the southward. At 4h. 30m. the America again tacked to the westward and laid 'well up' for the island.

The America reached in towards the island, distant from Nab two miles and a half, the Titania keeping her reach to the southward and westward and was now 'half mainsail down.' At 5h. 30m. 15sec. the America having passed us, and brought the Nab to bear from her S.W., was timed as the winner. Unfortunately, there was no gun on board to give either of the vessels a welcome, and a little smoke and steam from 'the big tube' of the steamer was all that could be resorted to.

The match was so far at an end, and the America stood on for Cowes, steering in for Brading, and then reached to the northward; from thence she again tacked, fetched in under Fishbourne, went about again, and after making another short tack, went to her moorings in Cowes Roads.

At 5h. 57m. the Titania was seen making towards the steamer she having been nearly out of sight. After reaching in towards the island to the southward of the 'Princessa,' she tacked to the northward, and at 6h. 22m. 15sec. having reached the proper bearing, she was thus timed as arriving at the goal, being exactly 52 minutes behind the America out and home, which gives 4m. 12sec. in favour of the America for the run 'dead before it,' and 47m. 48sec. over her adversary in working back against a strong wind.

Writing to Colonel Hamilton, the day after the race, Lord Wilton made the racing season for the *America* complete:

I must congratulate you upon the success of the America yesterday which was complete. I enclose you the stakes that were deposited with me before the race. My address in London is 7 Grosvenor Square. I

> must now bid you farewell as I leave this station for London today, but I hope the period will not be far distance when I shall have the pleasure of seeing you again. I beg that you will kindly convey my adieus to the Commodore and his brother

Whilst the speed of *America* was once again proven and the undoubted seamanship and skill of Old Dick Brown and his crew unquestioned, still a persistent doubt lingered in the minds of the beaten establishment in Cowes.

One terrific story, ahead of the race against the *Titania* – indeed some days before, albeit unconfirmable is of the Marquess of Anglesey docking his boat – The *Pearl* – nearby off Cowes Roads and paddling over to the *America*, incidentally with James Steers who had been sailing with him that day, whilst she lay at anchor. After introducing himself and being warmly greeted, the Marquess made a beeline to the aft of *America* and, determined to see first-hand whether she had a propeller, lent over so far that Commodore Stevens had to prevent him from falling overboard by grabbing hold of his wooden leg. The Marquess was brought back onboard but the propeller story lingered right up until dry dock in Portsmouth where clearly the rumour was just that.

Explaining the speed of the *America* became something of an obsession in the journals of the day, with the invincible narrative enhanced by the resounding win over the *Titania* amplifying the victory in the race around the Isle of Wight. British yachting was smarting whilst in *America*, news of the win and the resounding pride in the shipbuilding industry of the New World had not yet broken.

A rather distinguished Royal Naval Officer who had served on the *Pearl*, the *Waterwitch* and the *Daring* ships wrote to *The Times* where a special column entitled 'Shipping Interest' provided the perfect platform for his detailed comments, which were published on August 29 1851. Captain H. J. Matson's letter attempted to dissect the merits of the *America*, her hull form, sails and general form. It is an accurate take on the feelings of the more informed of the British yachting scene, and a far cry from the media-enhanced version of the events:

> Sir, – It is quite refreshing after all the nonsense lately written on the subject, to read your remarks of this morning on the 'shipping interest,' particularly those having reference to our late defeat in the waters of the Solent. Many attempts have been made to lessen the significance of that defeat, by asserting that our yachts are built exclusively for comfort and

not for speed. This I positively deny. In many cases, owners of yachts have been willing to sacrifice everything for speed and have given the builders a carte blanche to that end; some have just now given up their vessels to the builders to experimentalize upon, by lengthening their bows, which will greatly increase their tonnage but make little or no difference in the accommodation. It is not fair to our wealthy and public-spirited owners of yachts, or to our American rivals, to assert that our builders have not had ample opportunities to produce the fastest vessels which their experience and ingenuity could devise, unfettered by any conditions whatever. It is quite a mistake to suppose that speed and capacity are incompatible with each other: those qualities are combined in every Yankee merchantman. The America, although a 'Flying Dutchman,' is no phantom ship. She is a good substantial craft, fit to go to sea in any weather with perfect ease and safety. She has fair accommodation, and would doubtless have had more, had her builder guessed the sort of vessels she would have to contend with. During a six-year service on the coast of North America I have had abundant opportunities of seeing what such vessels can do in the heaviest weather.

The America appears to be built on scientific principles; her form gives her extreme stability, for which she is in no way dependent on her ballast. With our yachts it is generally a mere question of 'canvas v. ballast.' This must be patent to all who have witnessed the hideous sight of a lot of yachts (I allude particularly to those of the Thames Club), burying themselves under a press of canvas, and heeling over to an angle of 45 degrees. The America sails very nearly on an even keel and has never been seen to heel over sufficiently to cause her to derive any considerable assistance from ballast. It is not, I trust, necessary to explain that ballast does not give any material stability to a vessel until she has a considerable heel. I do not advocate the propriety of building vessels to sail without ballast. Such can never be safe in a heavy sea. It has nearly proved fatal to several of Sir William Symonds' – the Quail, Star, Racer, etc, which were all thrown on their beam-ends by the force of the waves without a sail being set, at least nothing more than a trysail. A ship dependent solely on her form for stability is in this predicament: her form merely tends to keep her hull perpendicular to the surface of the element on which she floats; when, therefore, she may be floating on the side of a huge wave, rising at an angle of 45 degrees she becomes suddenly thrown over to that inclination and should a second wave give her a lift at this critical moment, before she has time to recover her upright position, and when the top weight of guns and the leverage of the masts all help to turn her over, a capsize would be a very probable result.

The ballast of a ship, however, acts in a totally different manner; it tends to attract the keel of the vessel to the centre of the earth, without any reference to the action of the waves. The America possesses both these essentials; her form gives great stability, and ballast renders her independent of the freaks of old Neptune.

In a letter you kindly published before the great challenge match came off, I expressed the opinion that much of the superiority of the America was due to the cut and make of her sails. This has been fully confirmed by the result and by all who have since written on the subject. Although the Titania was beaten by only four minutes in a run of 2.5 hours, she took nearly one-fourth longer time than the America to work the same distance to windward. Such an enormous disparity could not exist - ceteris paribus - between vessels with the respective forms of the America and Titania. It could only be occasioned by some erroneous application of the propelling power. The effort of our schooner and cutter sailors appears to be to spread the greatest possible amount of canvas on a given length of mast, which is then supported by all manner of ropes. The Americans are content with as much canvas as the stick will bear, without any material support from rigging. I cannot farther explain this without the use of a technical term, which I wish as much as possible to avoid.

In endeavouring to point out what appear to be some errors in our yachting system, I have not the slightest intention of casting ridicule on those to whom we are indebted for almost every improvement in the build and rig of our ships. Sir William Symonds, who has immortalised himself by bringing into the Navy a very superior class of sailing ships, began his career as an amateur builder of boats and yachts, and he has been eclipsed only by another yacht builder, Joseph White, of Cowes. The fastest merchantman I ever met at sea the Haidee, of London, was built by White. The fastest of the experimental brigs, the Daring, was also built on his lines, and her capacity for stowage was greatly superior to either of her competitors. The Phaeton has just left the frigate squadron covered with laurels. It was a long time before our dockyard artificers could make a fore and aft sail; consequently, the boom mainsails of our brigs were made by contract by a yacht sailmaker at

> Gravesend. My own first lessons in sailmaking, which I have since endeavoured to turn to account, were given by a noble yachtsman, and I believe there are few naval officers who have not picked up a wrinkle from the same source. I am, Sir, your very obedient servant. H. J. MATSON, Capt. R.N.

What Captain Matson so well described in his letter to *The Times* was anti-narrative, and it's quite something that it was indeed published. It needled the shipbuilding industry of Great Britain but also accurately picked up on the sail shape debate. The *America*'s spar-cleaved, flat-cut sails, designed for ultimate windward performance but small enough to enable handling in a breeze and a more upright hull-form in a combined wind and seaway, were a revelation to the British fleet's sagging flax. Almost certainly what Matson was alluding to here is that it was British sailmaking that needed to advance rather than hull form or design – an interesting analysis for the time.

Amidst the ongoing chatter around the *America*, she was quietly sold almost immediately after the race against the *Titania* to Lord John de Blaquiere, 4th Baron de Blaquiere of Ardkill, a captain in the West India infantry units of the British army. The sum that passed was reported to be the equivalent of $25,000, showing an uptick to the American syndicate owners on the original price secured with the W. H. Brown shipyard of $20,000. Perhaps this was in recognition of her two victories that summer and certainly a result of her new-found fame. Following the sale, the owners travelled smartly back to New York with a small profit after the expense of the Atlantic crossing, the win against the *Titania*, and with the 'RYS £100 Cup' in their possession.

John de Blaquiere, although a sporting type, was not a noted racing sailor, and having bought the *America*, and then subsequently mourning the suicide of his father just six weeks later, upon which he inherited the title of Hereditary Great Alnager of Ireland alongside the baronetcy, he took the yacht on a winter cruise of the Mediterranean. He then returned to the Solent the following year in 1852, hopeful of winning a hatful of races and securing his place in the yachting establishment.

Sailing the boat as he bought her, the *America* wasn't the rocket-ship that de Blaquiere had been led to believe by the breathless reporting in the national newspapers and journals. She struggled, most likely due to crew-handling not being as sharp as the American team that had sailed *America* across the Atlantic, in her first race against a fleet including the 60-foot cutter *Mosquito* and the now lengthened cutter *Arrow*, which came in at 79 feet. In a moderate airs race, *America* had her moments, particularly on reaching legs in the free and open waters around the back of the Isle of Wight, but when back in the Solent, she was overtaken on a course that led to Lymington in the west before heading back to Cowes. Both the *Arrow* and the *Mosquito* diced for the lead, splitting the win by just one second in favour of the *Mosquito* with *America* trailing in third. Robert Underwood, the pilot of the 1851 race, whom de Blaquiere had kept as navigator, was sacked soon after.

The only other race that de Blaquiere competed in was against the schooner *Sverige*, owned by Nicholas Beckman from Stockholm, with a £100 wager at stake which was, on the face it, a success. Over a course again around the back of the Isle of Wight and out some 20 miles from the Nab Lightship and return, *America* clawed back into the race on the final leg as the *Sverige* overstood the Nab Lightship and suffered in a patchy breeze. *America* went on to win in the trial, but the issue was an old foe on the racecourse in the form of the *Wildfire* – the Irish cutter now racing under the flag of the Royal Victoria Yacht Club in Ryde that many believe beat the *America* (informally) in the race that mattered for the 'RYS £100 Cup'.

Again, the *Wildfire* was not a categorised entrant due to its shifting ballast, preferring to sail with the yachts over the course in an unofficial capacity, but reports suggest that in the beat to windward to a mark-boat 20 miles off from the Nab Lightship, she was some 15 minutes ahead at the turn before annulling her race and returning to Solent waters. This was enough for de Blaquiere, and he never raced *America* again, selling her in 1853 to Henry Montagu Upton, the 2nd Viscount Templeton who only sailed her for one season before laying her up in Cowes where she lay until 1859. A chequered history of the yacht thereafter is chronicled at length elsewhere with an eventual rebuild, a renaming to *Camilla* by the owner H. E. Decie in 1860, a scuttling in the American Civil War before resurrection again. She sailed again in the America's Cup trials in 1870 but never again attained the revered heights and fame that she so enjoyed in that summer of 1851 in Cowes.

For the syndicate members of the *America*, however, the return home was a triumph. News had reached Boston long before their arrival back and *The Lawson History* records the following:

> ... the news was received during a celebration at the statehouse of the opening of railway communication between the United States and the Canadian provinces. Daniel Webster was addressing a large audience in the hall of the House of Representatives he broke off in his speech to

announce the victory. 'Like Jupiter among the gods,' he said, 'America's first and there is no second.'

Upon their actual return, the syndicate members were entertained at a lavish dinner, held in their honour in the heart of New York at Astor House, a luxury hotel on the corner of Broadway and Vesey Street, often referred to as 'the best-known hotel in America.' With them, they brought the Cup, which standing at just 68.6 cm high was somewhat unremarkable in stature but mighty in significance. In an age where silverware was undergoing a renaissance of extremity as master silversmiths became ever more emboldened with their designs, the RYS £100 Cup stood as a stock piece of Victoriana and presented a conundrum to the seven, now aged, members of the syndicate.

Sometime later, the date is not recorded, George L. Schuyler's son, Philip Schuyler (also grandson of Colonel James A. Hamilton) revealed that the syndicate made fairly detailed plans to melt down the trophy and to cast medals commemorating the win with the date, venue and timing embossed on each casting. There were even ideas around framing the medals, or presenting them in velvet-lined boxes, but mercifully these plans came to nothing. The Cup stayed in the possession of the syndicate owners in rotation, regularly being their centrepiece at dinner parties and a most enlightening conversation-maker. The Cup still has those qualities today.

What to do with the trophy became a topic of debate once the afterglow of success and restored national pride had naturally died. In England, the shipyards were alive with new builds led by Lord Wilton who commissioned the 312-ton schooner *Zara* from White's in Cowes while the Ratsey yard built two schooners with Joseph Gee ordering *Gloriana* at 134 tons and Richard Naylor commissioning the 249-ton *Constance*. It is further recorded by the Royal Yacht Squadron that Lord Wilton commissioned George Steers to design him a schooner on the same lines as the *America* but this petered out and was never executed.

British yachting and shipbuilding reared back to life whilst over in New York, shipbuilding continued at pace. It was a brief decade of prosperity before the American Civil War broke out in 1861 largely over the persistent issue of slavery that was so mocked in the London journals during the Great Exhibition, with the characterisation sticking like glue, at least in the eyes of the cartoonists and satirists of the day, to anything referring to America, its dignitaries and politicians.

Some six years passed from the winning of the trophy before a decision was taken and although widely, and correctly attributed to George L. Schuyler, John Cox Stevens, a dying man in 1857 (he died on 10 June 1857), will almost certainly have had a hand in what was to come next. Schuyler's idea was that the Cup should be conveyed to the New York Yacht Club for its safe-keeping but primarily to promote international sporting competition. Such had been the social and cultural success of the *America* and its crew crossing the Atlantic that Schuyler and Stevens recognised the power that sport had to unite and so, on 8 July 1857, a smartly worded 'Deed of Gift' was presented alongside the Cup to those aims:

> Any organised Yacht Club of any foreign country shall always be entitled through any one or more of its members to claim the right of sailing a match for this cup with any yacht or other vessel of not less than thirty or more than three hundred tons, measured by the custom-house rule of the country to which the vessel belongs.
>
> The parties desiring to sail for the cup may make any match with the yacht club in possession of the same that may be determined upon by mutual consent; but, in case of disagreement as to terms, the match shall be sailed over the usual course for the annual regatta of the yacht club in possession of the cup and subject to its rules and sailing regulations – the challenging party being bound to give six months' notice in writing, fixing the day they wish to start. This notice to embrace the length, custom-house measurement, rig, and name of the vessel.
>
> It is to be distinctly understood that the cup is to be the property of the club, and not of the members thereof, or owners of the vessel winning it in the match; and that the condition of keeping it open to be sailed for by yacht clubs of all foreign countries upon the terms above laid down, shall forever attach to it thus making it perpetually a Challenge Cup for friendly competition between foreign countries.

Many parts of this 'Original Deed of Gift' still stand today but the trophy that was donated as 'America's Cup' was somewhat different when it arrived at the New York Yacht Club having been engraved on its most prominent bulbs in a mish-mash of script and fonts. The central bulb promotes the trophy most clearly as the '100 Guinea Cup' before listing details of the date and recording the win 'By Yacht America'.

On a panel below, today barely readable due to the fading of the inscription, are two lists divided into 'Cutters' and 'Schooners' that lists 13 competing yachts including the *Volante, Arrow, Alarm, Mona, Bacchante, Freak* and *Eclipse* in the 'Cutters' section, and the *Beatrice, Wyvern, Ione, Constance, Gipsy Queen,* and *Brilliant* in the 'Schooner' section. Quite why the *Aurora* was left off is a mystery. One further inscription of note, found on the bulb directly behind the original inscription on the 'reverse' of the trophy is the wording: 'Schooner America, 170 Tons, Commodore John C. Stevens, Built by George Steers of New York, 1851.' No mention of the Brown Shipyard that Steers was working for, and speculation on the reason behind this varies, but clearly Stevens demanded that Steers be recognised.

With America's Cup in place and accepted at the New York Yacht Club, a notice was sent on 21 July 1857 to all foreign clubs announcing the format and the Deed of Gift and inviting 'spirited contest for the championship' and promising 'all challengers a liberal, hearty welcome and the strictest fair play', a sentiment conveyed in sincerity but ultimately an empty promise as the early challengers would soon find out.

The American Civil War naturally dulled any enthusiasm for pleasure boating and racing so the competition for 'America's Cup' effectively sat on ice until its conclusion in 1865. The following year, yachting returned thunderously with the first Atlantic offshore race organised in the winter of 1866 between three American clippers that piqued interest in the media in Britain.

A *Times* report on the 27 December 1866 recorded:

> The Americans have once more done a thing never attempted by any other people. They have set three pleasure yachts to race against each other at headlong speed across the broad and stormy ocean, from New York to Cowes, and not content with the longest race, they have added to the daring feat by rewarding the victor with about the largest money prize ever proposed in such a contest. The Henrietta, the Vesta, and the Fleetwing started from New York at 1 p.m. on the 11th, and the first of the three which arrived at Cowes was to receive a prize of $90,000. The victory has been already won. At 6 40 p.m. on Christmas Day, the Henrietta appeared oft Cowes, having accomplished the passage from New York in fourteen days, four hours, and forty minutes. What this means the reader will understand when we say that the quickest passage across the Atlantic ever yet made by a sailing vessel was only performed in thirteen days and eight hours. In fact, the voyage would have been a fair one even for a powerful steamer. The umpire in the

match left New York in the Scotia and did not get here much too soon to see the winner appear. The two rivals of the Henrietta were only a few hours behind her.

No observer of American character will be surprised at the interest which this unprecedented contest excited on the other side of the Atlantic. For some days before the start, New York was alive with excitement, and the sensation was all the more intense from the very evenness of the match. It does not appear, indeed, that the Henrietta was the favourite. Odds were laid at the last minute on the Vesta, though the beauty and promise of the other two were thought astonishing. There is only one circumstance which may be supposed, perhaps, to explain the result. 'The eye of the master' is a potent spell, and the owner of the Henrietta took passage in her himself. The Vesta and the Fleetwing were entrusted to their respective captains, while their owners remained in New York; but the Atlantic Cable will have completed the marvels of the story, and the issue of the race will have been known in America as soon as it was published here. A communication despatched from our Government to the United States' Consul at Southampton is evidence not only of the interest taken in the event, but of the perilous character of the race itself. The Fleetwing, it will be observed, had six of her crew swept off by a sea in mid-passage. Admiral Pasley (Admiral Sir Thomas Sabine Pasley) was directed by the authorities to hold himself in readiness to offer the racing vessels the assistance of the Dockyard, and the compliment was deservedly paid not only to these representatives of a friendly and kindred people, but to the daring spirit of adventure in which the match had been conceived and executed. There is, indeed, no other such match on record. Some of our own merchantmen have occasionally raced against each other from China to England, but these were large clipper ships striving to get a few hours' start in the way of business ... The success, however, of the Henrietta is as complete as that of the 'America' a few years ago, and far more surprising. The 'America' was simply an example of new principles dexterously applied to shipbuilding; this ocean yacht race has brought high national qualities into play, but in both cases the Americans were true to their own pretensions and shot clear ahead of the Old World. It is remarkable that yachting, in which the Americans have thus excelled us, has always been regarded as the peculiar pastime of England, and it is true enough, no doubt, that in no country is the pursuit invested with so much favour and popularity. But our yachtsmen take things

> comfortably. We build our pleasure-boats really for pleasure and sail them for pleasure. An Englishman's yacht is his home, and the home often of his family, too, for weeks together, and considerations of convenience are allowed to preponderate in the design and equipment of the craft. The Americans are both less domestic and more adventurous. They want yachts which can do what no other yacht has ever done, and they get them. Perhaps the comforts of these vessels might not be exactly suited to our tastes, but they teach us something, nevertheless. It is well for progress that there is a nation which knows no trammels of routine and shrinks from no experiment, however hazardous or audacious. The Americans have always, and naturally, been distinguished for shipbuilding and seamanship. They have set us the example in half-a-dozen new models, and they are pursuing the same course now, but we shall, perhaps, not be wrong in considering this ocean yacht race as expressive of another and more general spirit which has been remarked for some time past as on the increase in the States. The Americans are fast becoming a sporting people. They are establishing races and conducting them as they are conducted in the Old World ... They have got all the qualities of sportsmen. They are adventurous, fearless, fond of excitement, persevering, and acute. What they can accomplish as well as design this very yacht race shows ... Probably few people expected to see the visitors so soon, but the public will certainly be pleased to hear that a suitable reception had been already designed, and that a grand entertainment will be given to the gentlemen on board the racing vessels on Monday next.

British yachting circles were warming up and being geed on by the media to accept the coming force of American shipbuilding and innovation in a sport where an almost divine right to superiority by the Old World had been challenged and defeated. Now with American boats back in their waters, albeit briefly, and pushing the sport forward, the British yachting establishment had to react. It would be another four years before this happened and another remarkable turn of events before 'America's Cup' was challenged for.

The lessons of the *America* were many. Most pertinent was that the New World was a coming force in the field where Britain had held an almost unquestioned, unchallenged, dominance. Complacency had crept into almost all facets of ship and yacht design, and related componentry.

Furthermore, the gentlemanly pursuit of racing sailboats, be that on the coastal waters of the Solent or around Great Britain, was no longer the gold-standard. The Naval cabal and echo chamber of blind belief that British ship design was better, faster and more advanced than anything, anywhere in the world, was dashed and required a reappraisal. British feelings had been hurt by the victory on 22 August 1851.

As John Scott Russell, originator of the wave-line theory and designer of the defeated *Titania,* said so astutely, 'This challenge of America to England was of incalculable benefit to England. America reaped a crop of glory. England a crop of wisdom. It was worth the loss of a race to gain so much.'

The International Yacht Race Cowes, the American yacht *Sappho* leads the British yacht *Cambria* around St. Catherine's Point on the Isle of Wight. Drawing published in *The Illustrated London News*, 27 May 1870.

CHAPTER NINE

AMERICAN VISIT TO THE SOLENT LAYS THE SEEDS FOR THE FIRST CHALLENGE

All Englishmen believe that, taken as a whole, the art of yacht-building received a great stimulus by the acknowledged victories of the America in 1851, and now equally hope and believe that the leading English yachts can hold their own against the world; but, America excepted, there are no yachts which we think stand any reasonable degree of success against our vessels of the last few years.[1]

With the trophy gone from British shores, delivered back to New York by John Cox Stevens and Colonel Hamilton, by steamship in September 1851, it wasn't immediately obvious what the future would hold. Nobody on either side of the Atlantic had a vision initially for what any future competition would look like or, indeed, how the importance of the R. & S. Garrard's ewer would be perceived.

That its loss hurt was not in doubt. The immediate challenge that Britain would build a boat in 90 days capable of beating the *America* was understandably a reaction to the immediate loss of both the Cup and the loss of British shipbuilding face and reputation. The passing of several years until Schuyler's Deed of Gift donation of the trophy to the New York Yacht Club arguably stoked a desire to settle the score, and this aligned with advances that the British sailing fraternity felt were being made.

What also played into the narrative was a new breed of extraordinarily wealthy industrialists, embodied by the railway heir James Lloyd Ashbury,

[1] Letter from James Lloyd Ashbury, the schooner yacht *Cambria*, south coast of Spain, 3 October 1868. To the President of the New York Yacht Club.

who saw it as a source of national pride to win the trophy back. The history of the America's Cup has thrown up the most swashbuckling and fascinating characters, captains of industry and titans of wealth and power, all arguably encapsulated and emulated in the blueprint of Ashbury.

After the division and infighting, the years following the race around the Isle of Wight for the 'RYS £100 Cup' saw a remarkable resurgence for racing with the Royal Yacht Squadron very much seated at the beating heart of British yachting, a position that it has held every since through to this day. Throughout the 1860s and 1870s, with the commissioned schooners beginning to be finished, around 30 of these ever larger and more impressive yachts competed in regattas off the mainly southern coasts of Great Britain, entertaining crowds and providing a glamorous backdrop for accompanying society functions. Cowes as a town was resurgent, with building work aplenty providing the villas and upmarket retailers that its wealthy denizens demanded, alongside an electric telegraph and even the first demonstration of the electric telephone to Queen Victoria at Osborne House in January 1878.

The economic expansion of Great Britain was exponential through the period 1850 to 1870. With the country becoming known as the 'workshop of the world' and the ever increasing demand for coal to power the great factories of industry, the railway networks expanded accordingly. Indeed it was as far back as June 1842 that Queen Victoria first boarded the carriage of a steam train at Slough Station and took the ride to London Paddington, becoming the first British monarch to ever ride a train.

Creating both rolling stock and iron work for this Victorian era of expansionism was the Ashbury Carriage and Iron Company, founded in Manchester by John Ashbury, which became a limited company in 1862. Joining his father's business at a young age was James Lloyd Ashbury, who rose through the ranks remarkably quickly becoming a manager at the age of just 21 with a controlling stake by the age of 30. However, tired of the incessant bad air quality from the coal-fuelled industries of Manchester, James moved to Brighton, in the early 1860s, and began sailing on a small cruising yacht on day trips during the summer months, more for the medicinal benefits of the crisp coastal air than out of a desire to sail or race competitively.

The death of his father in 1866 brought him a vast inheritance and James Lloyd Ashbury was suddenly a man about town with the resources to enter the burgeoning yachting scene in a big way. He could certainly see the societal benefits and chose Harwich, Suffolk, as his racing area and the Royal Harwich Yacht Club, where he would become Commodore in 1869.

But it was to Michael Ratsey, one of the foremost boatbuilders in Cowes, that he turned for his magnificent 188-ton (by Thames Measurement) ballasted schooner *Cambria*, described lavishly in *The New York Herald*, a widely read and influential paper between 1835 and 1924:

> She is a keel schooner, substantially built of oak, with teak topsides. Her interior fittings are remarkably beautiful, rich, and in good taste, and the wainscoting is finished in polished oak. On the principle upon which she was built the Cambria is a most perfect triumph, and no one need doubt that she is the finest schooner in Great Britain. All of the delicate niceties employed by English yachtsmen in ballasting, sparring, and canvassing, have been tested by Mr. Ashbury, who, with a spirit which does credit to the most fascinating of all pastimes, has done much to develop yachting among his own countrymen to its present high status.

And the journal continued:

> The Cambria has 21 tons of ballast smelted and run into her timbers, and she has also four tons of lead bolted to her keel. Under sail she spreads a vast area of canvas and works in the wind with the ease and facility of a weathervane. It is by her qualities of being sharp and quick in stays, of being close to the wind, of making good time in light airs that yachtsmen claim that she is one of the fastest schooners in the world. By the wind, that is close-hauled, she has gaff topsails bent to the ordinary spars; but in sailing free she has much longer and lighter and more flexible yards aloft, and the sail of lighter canvas, of course, clubs out a considerable distance. Her bowsprit is a very peculiar spar, and with the jib boom and flying jib boom is all in one stick and rigs in and out at the option of the sailing master. Of course it is ugly in appearance, but the nautical advantages claimed for it are many and doubtless well founded.

Launched in May 1868, *Cambria* was to become a firm favourite of the people of Cowes, proud of its build at the local yard of Michael Ratsey, although its owner was viewed as being somewhat of 'new money' and he raced under the burgees of both the Royal Harwich Yacht Club and the Royal Thames Yacht Club – indeed it was the latter with which he eventually challenged for 'America's Cup' in 1870, some 19 years after the first race and 13 since its gifting to the New York Yacht Club.

The summer of 1868 was the catalyst for a remarkable chapter in the history of the America's Cup and one that undoubtedly set the tone for the event through to the present day. Arriving in British waters that summer, again with the reputation that the *America* had enjoyed in 1851, was the *Sappho*, owned by Richard Poillon. It had been built at his shipyard, the 'C & R Poillon Shipwrights, Calkers & Spar Makers', in Bridge Street, Brooklyn, best known for their work on the clipper ships that plied their routes to the Far East, which had, during the American Civil War, built a number of gunboats for the US Navy.

Sappho had been launched in Brooklyn on 25 May 1867 and was worked up against the pilot cutters by Captain Tom Baldwin with a local crew. In 1868, she set sail across the Atlantic and was greeted on her arrival in Cowes with the same reverent and somewhat breathless fervour as her predecessor had been some 17 years earlier. Baldwin posted a challenge at the Royal Victoria Yacht Club, which was propagated with *The Times* newspaper picking it up on 18 August 1868, and reporting in full with the headline in capitals: AN AMERICAN YACHT CHALLENGE. ROYAL VICTORIA YACHT CLUB. RYDE, ISLE OF WIGHT.

> Mr Baldwin (Captain Tom Baldwin) has brought over from New York the American schooner yacht Sappho, of about 310 tons, and is desirous of trying her sailing qualities with some of the best English yachts. He proposes the following arrangements: A sweep stake of 20 sovs. entrance; time for tonnage, R.Y.S. scale, Thames measurement; course, once round the Isle of Wight, to start from off Cowes Castle. The course to be completed by the first vessel in nine hours, or less, or the racer to be void for that day, under the directions and by rules to be supplied by the Sailing Committee of the R.Y.S. The Aline, Cambria, Oimara, and Condor are especially invited to take part in this national race. In the event of their doing so, the Oimara to sail upon equal terms with the Sappho. The Condor to be placed in the scale of a vessel of 230 tons, the Aline and Cambria to be allowed time according to scale. No square sails to be carried, the Sappho having none; any fore and aft sails that may be desirable. The Sappho has a main-topmast staysail and jib topsail, besides the ordinary sails. No limit as to number of crew. Any other yacht will be allowed to enter. Cutters to have two thirds of their tonnage added, but no greater allowance of time will be allowed than 20 minutes. The 'Rules of the Road,' as contained in the R.Y.S. sailing directions will be adopted. It is proposed that the race

> shall he sailed on Tuesday next, the 21st. The vessels to be at their stations at 8a.m., and to start punctually at 9a.m. The entries to close 3 hours before the hour of starting and to be sent to the Secretary of the R. Y. S., Cowes Castle. All minor regulations will be supplied by the Secretary of the R. Y. S., in writing or print, to each vessel before 8a.m. of the day of the race. N.B. Should the day named be unfavourable, the race to be sailed on the first subsequent favourable day, as the vessels will not be started unless there is a probable chance of the race being completed within the time limit.

Billed as the 'race of the year', the passage around the Isle of Wight is worthy of a full airing here as it laid the foundations for the first British challenge by James Lloyd Ashbury two years later and a most full description was covered in the 'Sporting Intelligence' section of *The Times* on the 27 August 1868:

> The great yacht race of the year came off on Tuesday around the Isle of Wight in the match between the American schooner Sappho and the English schooners Aline and Cambria, and cutters Oimara and Condor. The Sappho is a new vessel, is reported to be the fastest in all weathers out of New York Bay, and may, therefore, be taken as representing the latest American ideas of yacht building and rig in the form of a fore and aft rigged schooner – a matter in which they have hitherto stood unrivalled. The yachts representing England were as worthy of the honour as was the Sappho that of representing America. The Aline has made a great reputation by her fleetness and general behaviour under canvas in all weathers. She was built by Camper and Nicholson, of Gosport, and is the best racing yacht the firm has yet sent afloat. The Cambria was built by Ratsey, of Cowes, and this is her first year afloat. Her owner, Mr. James Ashbury, in giving the order for her construction, gave it simply for a racing schooner to exceed 200 tons, leaving all matters connected with the lines of the vessel to the builder, and thus rightly throwing upon him the responsibility of her success or failure as a racer. The Cambria, therefore, represents the latest ideas of an English yacht builder, without any alteration from the original design to meet the views of the owner. The Oimara and Condor are both Clyde-built vessels, and of them it is enough to say that finer or swifter craft have not yet been seen in English waters, while, at the same time, their owners very rightly believe that no cutter afloat can equal them. The skill of both nations, therefore, was very fairly matched, and whichever side won the other would have no right to grumble. The

conditions of the race when the famous America 'whipped' the British yachts and carried off the Cup at Cowes in 1851 were very different from the present. Then, in the construction of a yacht, a builder's ideas of the form required for speed was in nine instances out of ten sacrificed to the owner's requirements for room and comfort inboard, and at the same time our builders of yachts were far behind American builders in all matters relating to the form of hull or clothing aloft required for a first-class clipper fore and aft schooner. This was a speciality of the Americans, and in this, as in many other things, they very justly boasted of licking all the world. While the New York Yacht Club in 1851 despatched to Europe to contest with us for our highest aquatic honours a vessel in which every consideration had been sacrificed in her construction to the one great desideratum speed, our yachtsmen entered upon the struggle with her in vessels whose chief characteristics were luxuriance in state and bed cabins, and old-fashioned European notions of form of hull. The easy victory of the American over all our yachts on every point of sailing was an abrupt but wholesome shock to our national prejudices and gave an impetus to yacht racing here that to the present time has lost none of its original force. This carrying away by a stranger of the prize cup of the year from Cowes to New York was too much even for our cool philosophy, and, as a result of this rough awakening yachts were laid up or sold, and orders flowed rapidly in upon our yacht builders for 'Americas.' It is somewhat astonishing that although the America had been seen and measured in dock in this country not one of them produced a craft at all like her when they got an order for a similar schooner and professed themselves able to produce one. The only vessel that was really a good return for the money bestowed upon her was the grand Alarm in her conversion by the late Mr. Weld to a schooner, and in the match of Tuesday there was a feeling of regret among yachtsmen that she was not present with her racing flag to share the responsibility of upholding the yachting honour of England.

So, matters stood on Tuesday morning as the Sappho took up her position for the start off the Royal Yacht Squadron Castle in Cowes Roads, in company with her English antagonists the Cambria, Oimara, Condor, and Aline, for a contest which had been looked forward to with a degree of interest unparalleled in yachting annals. One observation more before the race. We have drifted into a system of deep keels, lead ballast, and heavy spars. The Americans stand by comparatively shallow

> keels and light ballast and balance the powers of a vessel's hull by her canvas. For all seagoing purposes the Americans are right, and we are wrong; but with this qualification, that our yachts do not carry their racing spars and canvas on a sea voyage. For yacht racing in smooth waters, around such a course as the Isle of Wight, we must look to Tuesday's race for a solution of the problem.

After a slow start and what amounted to a nip and tuck cruise, the race came alive at St. Catherine's Point, the halfway mark for the race, with *The Times* picking up the story:

> At 3.45 p.m. the four English yachts were off St. Catherine's point, with the wind freshening, the tide slackening, and the Needles Rocks in sight ahead, 12 good miles distant. The Cambria tacked off short of the others off St. Catherine's, and when she tacked for her reach across the bay, she looked to leeward of the Needles. The Aline, Condor, and Oimara having stood further off, their bowsprits pointed to windward of the rocks when they tacked and promised them short work of it. But tack short or long, the Cambria was in good hands. A long reach was made into Freshwater Bay, the Oimara sailing to leeward of the lot and the Condor to windward. The Sappho had stood off from under Ventnor well to the southward and was now coming along under the strong breeze and through the biggish waves that were running between St. Catherine's and the Needles with great speed, through Chale Bay, but all that distance astern. About 4 p.m. the Oimara, Condor, Cambria, and Aline tacked and stood off on the starboard tack to enable them to weather the Needles, the two cutters and the Cambria being close together. All the four as they stood out on the same tack from under the vast limestone cliffs, lipping in the water over their lee rails and washing their stern heads with the waves meeting their bows, made a very pretty and effective marine picture. With a hand out on her bowsprit and in readiness to send in her jib and get out her ballooner the Oimara, as the leader, approached the Needles Rocks, which were weathered and helms put up for the run home to Cowes.
>
> The Sappho was too far astern of all to be timed with the others round the Needles, and was now, in fact, altogether out of the race. Under balloon jibs and big topsails and with booms raised well off on their starboard quarters, the yachts ran up against the tide, but before the still fresh breeze, for Cowes Roads, and, most undeniably, four other vessels of equal beauty and speed were never before seen together. Off Hurst

Castle the Cambria drew up close to the lee quarter of the Condor, when the latter, becoming alarmed, sent aloft a jib topsail as a check to the schooner's presumption; but by the time they were off Yarmouth the Cambria was abreast of her, and a gun fired from the shore told of the joy of Admiral Hamond at the success of the bold schooner. The Cambria and the two cutters, fighting their battle for a place, passed Yarmouth in mid-stream, running against the greatest strength of the tide, the Aline in the meantime hugging the island shore, and closing up fast. Soon afterwards the Cambria had the Condor under her stern, and then she was luffed in a little towards the island to cheat the tide as much as possible, and also to keep ahead of Mr. Sutton's schooner, which seemed about to perform her old trick of coming in with a rush to the front at the finish. All four vessels, under the conditions of a lee running tide, were now running with amazing speed, and the Cambria, although on one occasion given by accident the 'wash' from the Victoria Club steamer, outstripped the others, and drew up abreast of the leading vessel – the Oimara. At 5.40 pm., when the four English yachts were off Newtown, the American schooner hove in sight astern from them as she came round Sconce Point for Yarmouth Roads. After passing Newtown the wind veered from dead astern of the vessels to their port-quarters sufficiently to fill head sails, and as the Condor and Oimara felt the pull of their great ballooners and the magnificent Aline kept on her rush for the front, it became doubtful for a few minutes which vessel of the four would finish the race as the first vessel in. The Cambria, however, was not to be balked of the great honour she had so splendidly sailed for, and off the east end of Gurnard Bay took the lead unmistakably with every inch of canvas drawing, and entered Cowes Roads the winner, without time allowance, of the most important, interesting, and best-contested race of the present year.

The flag-boat off the Royal Yacht Squadron Castle at Cowes, the winning post for the race, was passed by the five yachts as they ran in from the westward, and the race concluded as follows: Cambria 6.17.30. Aline 6.19.36. Oimara 6 22 55 Condor 6.25.40. Sappho 7.55.0.

Admiral Sir Thomas Pasley, in his steam yacht the Fire Queen, Staff-Commander F. W. Paul, accompanied the yachts in their run up from Yarmouth to Cowes. The sailing yacht of Rear-Admiral G. G. Wellesley, C. B. and a whole fleet of private steam and sailing yachts also kept company as well as their respective speeds would allow. On

> the arrival of the yachts off the Royal Yacht Squadron Castle as they ran in at the finish every man, woman, and child in Cowes appeared to have congregated on the beach, baling with frantic cheers the success of the Cowes built craft – the beautiful Cambria. The defeat of the American schooner Sappho in so marked a manner must not be made too much of by us or taken as a fair test of the vessel's racing powers. The Sappho as a racing vessel, wants both more sail and ballast, and the loss of her jib-boom may also be said, independently of other reasons, to have thrown her in her then position out of the race and beyond any hope of recovery. Ballasted and fitted with canvas for racing more according to our notions on such matters, she would be a remarkably swift and powerful craft, and more especially so in such races as the Channel matches of the Thames and Victoria Clubs. On the whole, the Sappho although beaten by her English sisters, is not dishonoured by their victory.

With success in that race, the thought of challenging for the America's Cup came to James Lloyd Ashbury. If he could beat the Sappho, regarded as the fastest vessel in America, so convincingly, then surely, he could win back 'America's Cup', which he mistakenly referred to in subsequent correspondence as a 'Queen's Cup', and restore not only national nautical pride but seal his place in high society.

The New York Herald of the 19 November published the subjoined challenge given by Ashbury to the Commodore of the New York Yacht Club. The challenge contained a number of inaccuracies that underlined his misunderstanding, or non-recognition, of the terms of the Deed of Gift and of the stringent conditions that the New York Yacht Club, now the trustees, would implement which would honour both the spirit and letter of the document controlling America's Cup. Ashbury trying to dictate terms was not something the club would entertain.

The challenge was brazen, but made with initial good intention. What Ashbury would discover was a club determined to see off any challenge at all costs – something that would seep into their raison d'être for the next 132 years. Ashbury began: 'So far, matters have not been fully arranged, but it is hoped that nothing will be left undone to bring about an international race, wherein the true merits of competitors will be brought to the test.'

> The following are the terms of the challenge: Schooner Yacht Cambria, off South Coast of Spain October 3rd, 1868. To the President of the New York Yacht Club.

Sir, As the owner of the English schooner Yacht Cambria, which some time ago won the race round the Isle of Wight against the American schooner Sappho and three crack English vessels, I cannot but regret the accident to your representative vessel, and also my inability to have remained in England to again race her round the Wight or across to the coast of France. I am now on a cruise along the coast of Portugal and Spain, a journey which I postponed at great inconvenience in order to give me the pleasure of being courteous to the extent of allowing me to enter against so splendid a vessel as the Sappho, the property of an American gentleman; and I am in hopes this communication will show the owners of the Sappho that they may probably have an opportunity of again testing her qualities against the Cambria, and in American waters. All Englishmen believe that, taken as a whole, the art of yacht-building received a great stimulus by the acknowledged victories of the America in 1851, and now equally hope and believe that the leading English yachts can hold their own against the world; but, America excepted, there are no yachts which we think stand any reasonable degree of success against our vessels of the last few years. All yachtsmen, as well as others, duly appreciate the compliments your New York Club have paid us by, from time to time, sending vessels over to this country, and it is a source of much regret on this side of the water that those compliments have not been reciprocated by any leading yacht club deputing one on more of their crack vessels to go to New York waters for racing purposes. So much do I feel on this subject that I proposed to one of the leading clubs last winter to send to New York an invitation for two or three vessels to come over in time for the races at Cowes and Ryde this year, and then for several of our leading yachts to sail them back to New York; and, in order to tempt our friends over here, I proposed that special subscriptions should be solicited from each member of a yacht club wherewith to form a large fund for giving splendid prizes, irrespective of what the clubs might give. At the meeting in question, I offered to subscribe any sum up to 500 sovs. and to enter the Cambria for the return race to New York. I mention this in no egotistical spirit, but simply to show that I desire to fairly test the merits of my vessel against those of America in rough as well as smooth waters. Unfortunately, this arrangement could not be carried out, as most of the owners generally leave off yachting after the Wight races for grouse and partridge shooting or go abroad. Before my yachting time your schooner America had the honour of winning the cup presented by Her Majesty to the Royal Yacht Squadron, and I am led to believe that the New York yacht clubs have in the most friendly and courteous manner offered the cup in question to be sailed for in New York waters to any English yacht which will compete for it. It is an esteemed honour for any Englishman to win at any time the Queen's Prize, but I venture to think none would be so much valued as the one so triumphantly taken away in 1851 by the America, and subject to conditions which I hope will be deemed equitable and reasonable to all concerned. I now have the pleasure to ask you to kindly state to your committees that I am disposed to challenge all America for the possession of the cup in question.

Firstly: I propose that during or before the season of 1869 the New York Yacht Club select their champion schooner of a tonnage not to exceed 10 percent, of the Thames measurement (188 tons) of the Cambria.

Secondly: The vessel referred to I would desire to see arrive in England in ample time to take part in the matches of the Royal Yacht Squadron at Cowes and the Royal Victoria Yacht Club at Ryde, for which races she will doubtless be permitted to enter, on time allowance and measurement as per rules of those clubs. These races are held early in August, six to eight or nine in number, round the island (60 miles), the Victoria and Queen's courses (also about 60 miles), and probably a run to Cherbourg and back. The prizes would be the annual Queen's Cup, presented to the Royal Yacht Squadron; two cups of £10 each from the towns of Cowes and Ryde, and several £100 and £50 cups; and, I may add, that If the yacht could arrive about a month earlier, she would be in time for some of the best ocean races of the Royal Thames Yacht Club.

At these races your representative vessel would meet all the best and fastest English and Scotch yachts – among others, schooners Guinivere, Alarm, Cambria, Aline Egeria, Gloriana, Albertine, Blue Bell, Pantomime, Gelert etc.; yawls Lufra and Kulia; cutters Oimara, Condor, Fiona, Arrow, etc. – and would have a fair opportunity of testing her qualities during the height of the Isle of Wight yachting season, and with the temptation of so many prizes highly valued and much sought after, but not for their mere intrinsic value.

> Thirdly: On or about the 1st of September I would race your vessel from the Isle of Wight to New York for a cup or service of silver, value £250; no time allowance, and no restrictions as to canvas or number of hands.
>
> Fourthly: I would then, at an early date race the said vessel round Long Island, on the Royal Thames Yacht Club measurement, and their time allowance; two races out of three over this course to decide as to the championship and the final possession of the America's Queen's Cup of 1851, if I lost I would present the New York Yacht Club, or the owner of the successful vessel, with a cup, value 100 guineas; or I would race any other schooner of about my tonnage over the same course on the said conditions, the competing vessel to have been previously pronounced by the New York Yacht Club as the fastest vessel in America of her size and class and providing the said vessel had not been built since the date of this communication, and was in all respects a sea-going vessel and not a mere shell or racing machine. At your earliest convenience I shall be glad to hear from you or the club secretary on the subject. Meanwhile, believe me, yours truly, James Ashbury.

Correspondence continued through 1868 and into the early part of 1869. The New York Yacht Club was unwilling to entertain the suggestion of ocean races but accepted a challenge for 'America's Cup' only under the strict terms of the Deed of Gift of 1857. This was not to be cast aside or superseded by any new terms, especially those laid out by a challenger.

A point that exercised Ashbury most vehemently, when faced with a fleet of boats highly optimised for New York waters, was the use of centre-boarded yachts able to sail closer inland in tidal conditions. Back and forth correspondence between the New York Yacht Club and Ashbury did little to resolve the issue, with Ashbury maintaining that 'The cup having been won at Cowes, under the Rules of the R.Y.S., it thereby follows that no centre-board vessel can compete against the *Cambria* in this particular race.' The New York Yacht Club listened to the argument, as this was the first challenge so the power of the Deed of Gift was unproven, and reverted to the exact wording of the second paragraph of George L. Schuyler's cleverly worded document:

> The parties desiring to sail for the cup may make any match with the yacht club in possession of the same that may be determined upon by mutual consent; but, in case of disagreement as to terms, the match shall be sailed over the usual course for the annual regatta of the yacht club in

> possession of the cup and subject to its rules and sailing regulations – the challenging party being bound to give six months' notice in writing, fixing the day they wish to start.

The key line here was 'the match shall be sailed over the usual course for the annual regatta of the yacht club in possession of the cup and subject to its rules and sailing regulations,' and to this end Ashbury's desires were dashed. The New York Yacht Club would thus not disqualify any yacht qualified under *its* rules and regulations.

In particular, the club's committee paid scant attention to Ashbury's suggestion that the race for the Cup be a one-on-one match, as stated in the fourth part of his original challenge communication. This was never clarified explicitly, and it laid the foundations for a bitter first challenge and defence in 1870, the rumblings of which would last well into the second Ashbury challenge of 1871.

Depiction of James Lloyd Ashbury in *Vanity Fair*, 31 October 1874.

CHAPTER TEN

CAMBRIA'S DREAM AND BRITISH HOPES COME TO NAUGHT

The President of the United States (General Grant) did our friend the honour to breakfast with him on board the Cambria, and that is good enough testimony that no jealousy was created by the yacht race.[1]

Having failed in his attempt to enter the British Parliament as member for Brighton, Sussex, in 1868, the first election after the passing of the Second Reform Act of 1867, James Lloyd Ashbury's challenge proposed for 'America's Cup' in 1869 did not come off, but as a sportsman he was determined to make it happen the following year, despite a worrying drop in racing form.

Sappho had remained in English waters and, during the summer of 1869, had scheduled three races against *Cambria*, two of which she won with ease and the third, a race to Cherbourg in France and return, she declined to sail as the wind was on the beam and therefore sat outside the stipulations for a windward/leeward course. The secret to *Sappho*'s success was almost certainly due to modifications made in the winter of 1868, overseen by the untrained but brilliant yachtsman Captain Robert 'Bob' Fish, with the boat being 'hipped' and made wider amidships to produce a more powerful hull, although several accounts also suggest that she was far better sailed and handled than *Cambria*.

More worryingly for Ashbury were the results from the rest of the summer season in 1869 with a detailed account made by an observant scribe in *Hunt's Yachting Magazine*, sometime later in 1871. This recorded the *Cambria*'s

[1] Sir John Cordy Burrows, Mayor of Brighton, speaking at a dinner given in Ashbury's honour in January 1871.

racing season starting on the east coast of Britain with an opening race from the New Thames Club to Harwich in June 1868, where she came third, followed by a Royal Thames Yacht Club-organised schooner match a few days later which also saw her finish third. In a straight match-race, organised by the Royal London Yacht Club the day after, against the 170-foot schooner *Egeria*, she lost. In two further subsequent racing days, organised by the New Thames and Royal Thames Yacht Clubs, she was beaten again. Finally, it wasn't until she went 'offshore' in the Harwich Town Cup from Dover to Boulogne, and back again, that the first victory for *Cambria* was recorded.

Unabashed, or perhaps unknowing of the speed deficiency of *Cambria*, Ashbury's desire to race the American fleet came to a head through a friendship with James Gordon Bennett Jr., himself also an heir to a business fortune through his father's founding of *The New York Herald*. Bennett, like Ashbury, was a keen sportsman widely credited with bringing both tennis and the sport of polo to the United States. As a keen yachtsman, Bennett had ultimately been the winner of the pioneering offshore race across the Atlantic, in 1866, on his clipper *Henrietta*. In April 1867, Bennett purchased what was then the *L'Hirondelle*, owned by S. Dexter Bradford Jr., a Forsyth & Morgan schooner that had been built the previous year at Mystic Bridge, Connecticut. Renaming her *Dauntless*, Bennett brought the boat across to Queenstown in Ireland, in the summer of 1869, and Ashbury and Bennett did their best to arrange for a transatlantic race back to Sandy Hook in the early autumn, but owing to a refit, *Dauntless* was forced to decline at the last minute.

At the same time, late in 1869, Ashbury's communication with the New York Yacht Club became more focussed and centred around the Atlantic race happening in the March of 1870. In his letters to the club, which were met once again with both bemusement and amusement by the club, Ashbury stipulated that the races should be held in May with a triangular course from 'Staten Island, forty miles out to sea and back'. This was, however, viewed as unfavourable for the New York Yacht Club fleet. The insistence by the club that a yacht arrived having crossed the Atlantic 'on its own bottom' most likely guarded against the eventuality of a challenger being optimised for specific conditions. It was the start of the skewering-in-their-favour approach that the club took to the America's Cup.

Furthermore, Ashbury also wanted to exclude centre-boarded yachts, popular with the New York Yacht Club members at the time, and perfect for their coastal, shallow waters and also informed the New York Yacht Club that he intended to challenge for the America's Cup from 'one of the several Royal clubs' to which he belonged and that his preference was the Royal Thames Yacht Club to whom he would present the trophy if he won. He was also seeking to change the rules of the competition to become an offshore sailing event. Writing to the club he suggested that it should 'be held as a challenge cup, open to any royal or first-class recognised yacht club to compete for; providing six months' notice is given, and the course not less than 300 miles in the Channel or any other ocean.' The New York Yacht Club, smarting from the indignity of Ashbury trying to change the rules and dictate terms, reverted to the Deed of Gift on this and the requests were denied, but the straight challenge for the trophy accepted.

The agreed date for the America's Cup racing, however, was postponed to August and on 4 July 1870, *Cambria* and *Dauntless* set off on what would be a controversial race from Daunt Rock, south of the resort of Fountainstown, on the western side of Cork Harbour, to Sandy Hook, New York, dubbed in the British media as 'The Atlantic Yacht Race'. From the start, strategies very much differed with the *Cambria* taking a northerly route whilst the *Dauntless* dived south – indeed from the first night, the two never saw each other again throughout the race. *Cambria* won, albeit only just and the Reuters telegraph recorded on 27 July 1870 that:

> The Cambria arrived at Sandy Hook Lightship this afternoon at seven minutes past 3 and is the winner of the Atlantic Yacht Race. She was met down the river by a large number of yachts and steamers and was enthusiastically cheered the whole way up to Staten Island. The Dauntless arrived an hour and a quarter afterwards, but the yachts never sighted each other after the night of the start. This fact was owing to the Cambria taking a northerly course, reaching as high as 55 N., while the Dauntless kept the southern track. The Cambria carried away two foretopmasts but had spare ones on board to replace them. She met no other mishap and arrived at New York all well. She had strong westerly winds and fresh gales to Cape Race, which she sighted on Monday, the 18th. After that she had light headwinds to Sandy Hook. The Dauntless had a succession of strong north-west winds, with occasional gales and calms.

In New York, the victory by the English yacht was greeted with disbelief, but the story of the race unfolded in the coming days with reports of the loss of two crew overboard on the *Dauntless* in horrendous conditions, washed off the deck. *The Times*, in London reported the race in curt tones on 28 July 1870:

> The Cambria's time was 23 days 5 hours 17 minutes; that of the Dauntless 23 days 7 hours. Both vessels encountered very heavy weather. On the 7th of July the Dauntless lost two of her crew overboard in a gale and spent three hours in fruitless efforts to save them. On the 10th she lost a jibboom in a squall. The yachts were received at Sandy Hook by the entire yacht squadron of the New York, Atlantic, Brooklyn, and other yacht clubs. The weather was fine.

Ashbury was crestfallen by the loss of the crew members, and it was again reported, sometime later, indeed quite sometime after the actual race for the America's Cup, that he intended to make good for the families. These losses of crewmembers, as had also happened in the Atlantic Race of 1866, where six crew members were washed off the bow of the *Fleetwing*, were the collateral damage of sporting endeavour, although deeply and honestly felt by the swashbucklers instigating the progression of yacht racing.

On 19 August 1870, the following was reported in *The Times* in London with the Americans still smarting from defeat by an English yacht:

> Then the hope arose uppermost that there might be some irregularity in the management of the Cambria, which would give the race to the Dauntless by a foul, and in that case the national honour, as represented by the American yacht, would not be so greatly humiliated. There were, even late in the afternoon, men who would not believe that the British yacht had won, and who placed no faith either in the bulletins or in the despatches printed in the evening papers. They seemed to think that it was impossible that anything which floated in the shape of a yacht could beat the American vessel and had all manner of excuses for resisting the conviction that the Dauntless had indeed lost the victory ... Measures will be taken for the relief of the families of the two sailors who were washed overboard from the Dauntless. Mr. Ashbury has signified his intention of giving them each a purse.

The actual race for the America's Cup was run on the 8 August 1870, and over a typical course of the New York Yacht Club's annual regatta, as stipulated in the Deed of Gift. This was rigorously enforced by the New York Yacht Club who, in this first defence, fielded a fleet of yachts, which was bitterly opposed by Ashbury, including centre-boarders. In many ways, the first defence of the Cup set a precedence for what was to come, most notably that it was now to be a race around marker buoys, but its format to a 'match' pitting vessel against vessel would require some wise-headed thinking by the New York

Yacht Club and George L. Schuyler before the second defence. Returning to the New York fleet with much misty-eyed nostalgia was the revamped *America* and the *Sappho* who also contested the race, which was entered by a total of 25 yachts with 18 starting the race.

The harbour was filled with spectator craft and the concentration was most acute around the match-up between the *America, Cambria* and *Dauntless* with much national pride resting on the shoulders of the sailors of each. In a stable southerly breeze, at 11.26 am, the starting gun was fired with the 18 yachts lined up at anchor. The *Cambria,* having been given the choice of starting station, elected the innermost but one position. To New York salts this was a fatal decision with the wind switching to a more easterly direction, and as the yachts set their vast acres of canvas, *Cambria* was left trailing and was almost the last to get away, agonisingly stuck on the inside.

Building a lead that she would never relinquish was the 79-foot, 92.2-ton centre-boarded schooner *Magic,* owned by Franklin Osgood which had been completely rebuilt and modified for racing in 1869 by the shipbuilder David Carll at his yard on City Island. An unremarkable racing pedigree until her refit, *Magic* proved to be slippery, winning the race over *Dauntless* by 1 minute and 29 seconds – which was amplified on corrected time, relegating *Dauntless* to fifth in the fleet, whilst the *Cambria* arrived eighth on actual time and tenth on corrected. The *America,* the darling of the fleet, finished fourth. Describing the skipper of the *Magic,* the *New York Herald Tribune* characterised him by saying: 'Mr. Franklin Osgood, owner of the Magic, is a brave, courageous and bold seaman. He goes for every stitch of canvas aloft in a stiff breeze and would himself get in the weather rigging if it would accelerate the Magic's speed.'

J. D. Jerrold Kelley, writing in *American Yachts* (1884), gave a thrilling and rich account of that first race which attracted significant public interest in the spectacle:

> The public prayer being for any yacht to beat the representative of the Royal Thames Yacht Club, but best of all that it might be the America ... guns roared, men cheered, bells rang, and bands burst into loud and brazen notes of triumph; and when the Magic rounded the lightship, making it almost a certainty that the Cup was safe, there arose a shout painful in its intensity of delight, for it was the relieved outcome of pent-up excitement which had reached its culmination at this very point ... But the strength and beauty of the struggle was soon consummated by

a glorious victory, for as the 'Magic' rushed across the line it was not only in the fastest time ever made over the course, but all things considered, with the greatest victory to her record ever won by a yacht since the world was young.

A more detailed account appeared in *The Times* on the 5 September 1870:

People in England will fail to realize the extraordinary interest taken by Americans in the visit of the Cambria to this side of the world. The match yesterday for the Squadron Cup – by the way, it may be mentioned that the cup is persistently miscalled the 'Queen's' Cup - won by the America in 1851, with regard to the interest it excited quite eclipsed anything of the kind ever witnessed in England. The newspapers were full of the subject from the time of the arrival of the Cambria to the hour of the race, and in some cases most ridiculous accounts of the vessel and her owner appeared. The day after her arrival she went into the navy yard by permission of Admiral Porter, where, comparatively unmolested, her rigging was overhauled, and her cabins put in order. A few days afterwards she went on a lifting dock by one of the wharves, and then thousands crowded on board to get a peep of the extraordinary stranger. A new suit of cotton sails was fitted to her, and on Thursday, the 4th, she was towed to Staten Island ready for the race on the 8th. Unfortunately, excepting for a few hours, nothing but calms prevailed, so no opportunity was presented for her to be got under way for the purpose of stretching her new sails. On the Sunday most of the yachts that were to do battle for the retention of the Cup in America were at anchor around the Cambria, off the Club-house. They are all vessels with very low hulls, long sharp bows, extremely taut spars, and rigging and gear so light that one began to wonder if it could ever hold on, excepting in the very faintest of topsail breezes. Many of the yachts are painted white and carry centre boards; their hulls are shallow and the accommodation below, in comparison to the deck room they have, is much inferior to that of any English yacht. A few are heavier rigged, and look like sea-going yachts, but the majority certainly appear as if they would be most uncomfortable craft in a sea-way. The course chosen by the New York Yacht Club is exactly suited to these gossamer rigged craft, and such vessels as the Dauntless, Cambria, Fleetwing etc, had but a small chance of beating such a mosquito fleet.

The committee appointed to carry out the arrangements for the match courteously gave the Cambria choice of position, and the Cambria as a matter of course on the morning of the race took what appeared to be the weather berth, but before the hour appointed for the start the wind shifted, and the Cambria after all got the worst station in the fleet.

The measurement in square feet is arrived at by multiplying the greatest length on the water line by the greatest beam wherever found. Upon this measurement a table of time allowances is framed regulated by the duration of the race. The course was from Staten Island down the river, round Sandy Hook Lightship, and return to Staten Island – 37 miles – a course very similar to that on the Thames from Gravesend round the Nore light and back. At the time of the start hundreds of steamboats, crowded with spectators, were under way shrieking their whistles by way of compliment to the yachts. This is entirely an American idea, and we trust, for the sake of our ear, it will never be introduced into England. At first, we viewed these steamers with suspicion, and began to wonder if they would not crowd on the yachts and impede their progress; but nothing of the kind occurred, the whole of the steamers without exception keeping astern or well to leeward out of the yachts' way. The American yachts were regaled by the bands on board the steamers with 'Yankee Doodle,' and the Cambrians were flattered to hear 'God save the Queen,' amid the general din of steam whistles, shouting, and music.

At first it was agreed that the yachts should, according to the New York Yacht Club rules, set all canvas except head sails, but a few minutes before the start one of the committee rowed alongside the Cambria and said her sails must be lowered, as the arrangement now was to start them with all canvas down. This looked like giving the small craft an advantage, but no complaint was made by any of the large ones.

At 11.21 the gun was fired for the start. The Alarm was to windward, and next to her came the Calypso (centre-board), the Widgeon (centre-board), the Sylvie (centre-board), the Magic (centre-board), the Dauntless, the Tarolinta, the Halcyon (centre-board), the Idler (centre-board), the Rambler, the Madgie (centre-board), the Phantom (centre-board), the Fleetwing, the Madeleine (centre-board), the America, the Tidal Wave, the Cambria, and the Alice. The Magic was the first to slip and get her canvas up, and, bounding away, was soon clear of the whole fleet. The America, wonderfully quick in feeling her canvas, was the next to draw out, and these were rapidly followed by the Sylvie, Phantom, Idler, and Dauntless. The Cambria, considering the weight of her gear, made a very good start, and the Alarm and Tarolinta very bad ones. It was nearly a dead beat against a light breeze from south, course south by east through the Narrows, three miles. The twelve windward vessels started on the port tack, and the others, with the Cambria, on the starboard. All sent up balloon main-top-sails, and the Cambria made three ineffectual attempts to get up her fore-top-sail, but what with being hampered by the yachts that started on the port tack, two of whom in the first board she had to bear up for, and lubberly management it seemed that she was destined to sail without any fore-top-sail throughout the day. The American yachts apparently set to fore-top-sail in beating to windward, as for vessels having a standing preventer fore-top-mast backstay such a sail would be most inconvenient, if not impossible, to work. In the third board the Cambria on the starboard tack met the Rambler and Tarolinta on the port tack, and both refused to give way for her; the Cambria thus bore up to go under the Rambler's stern, and pass ahead of the other if possible; but this could not be done, and the Tarolinta, seeing that she was likely to be cut down – the Cambria could not bear up enough to clear her and could not go about without fouling the Rambler – put her helm a-lee and shot up in the wind. It was a pity she did not conform to the well understood 'rule of the road at sea' before; as it was, she came aboard of the Cambria, striking her on the port bow and carrying away a fore-shroud, fore-top-mast backstay, and springing the port arm of the fore crosstree. Twice after this the Cambria had to bear up for vessels, and it seemed that as long as this lasted in the short boards that were being made, she would never head anything in the match unless she cut everyone down that so unjustifiably made her bear up. The Dauntless made a very smart start, and her crew deserved some praise for, getting such a large vessel clear of the ruck in the narrow water. She certainly had a better position than the Cambria for the start, still we could not help admiring the smartness of her handling. The Magic, as one might expect to see the Flying Cloud or Gloriana do at home, was round and feeling her canvas while some of the others were thinking about it, and, having a good weather berth, was able to get through the Narrows in a board less than the Cambria. The latter at last, finding it so difficult working in such a crowd, made a longer stretch over under Fort Richmond, where she met a hotter tide but a clear course. When she tacked, she weathered the Rambler, Tarolinta, Alarm, Alice, and Widgeon, having previously been last of all. The course now altered to

S ’W. to the S.W. Spit Buoy, six and a half miles, and the water being broader, they fetched it in two boards.

The Cambria, now with a fore-top-sail set and fairly settled down to work, began to inspire those on board with more confidence in her powers, but we could all plainly see she had, no chance against such fleet rivals over a short river course. She in rapid succession weathered the Madeleine, Fleetwing, Halcyon, Calypso, and Tidal Wave, and seemed in a fair way of overhauling some of the others on her reach at the Lightship, nine miles distant. But scarcely had she passed the S.W. Spit when the wind drew out from S.E. by S., and instead of standing to the Lightship with sheets checked, as she would have done with wind from S., she had to keep close-hauled and make another board. The Magic, Idler, Dauntless, America, Phantom, and Sylvie were more fortunate, and fetched close round the Lightship, in spite of a strong lee tide, in one board from the S.W. buoy.

They bore up round the Lightship for the run home. In the long reach from the S.W. buoy the Dauntless had got up her main-top-mast staysail, and now supplemented it with a jib topsail; all the others, including the Cambria, doing the same. The wind freshened from S. E., sheets were got aboard a bit, and the Cambria commenced leaving those astern, and closing up with those in front hand over hand, the Dauntless, too, passing the Idler and making a hot chase after the Magic. But the latter had got the bit between her teeth and was so near the goal that nothing but a miracle would enable either of the others to get anything but a stern view of her. The Cambria’s chance of making a respectable finish was completely annihilated off the Hook Point, 14 miles from home, by her foretopmast carrying away; the clip hooks of the preventer backstay had broken, and that, with the crippled cross trees, let the mast go by the board. By this accident the Cambria lost fore-top-sail and jib-top-sail and, square sails being disallowed, she was obliged to continue the run home with ordinary fore-and-aft canvas, including a balloon jib.

Thus ended this memorable contest; no one will contend that it was one in all respects satisfactory; it proved no more than we already knew – that small boats of light draught of water, and lightly rigged, are better adapted to river sailing than large sea-going yachts. Mr. Ashbury sailed in the match as a representative of the Royal Thames Club, and had he

> been fortunate enough to have won the cup, that Club would have held it until again challenged for. On Thursday the whole fleet of yachts started from Glencove to sail down Long Island, around 85 miles to New London. A fine wind abaft the beam prevailed, and the Cambria beat the whole fleet, all racing and trying their utmost to be in first.

Coming ashore, Ashbury made mention of being fouled by the *Tarolinta* but with no recourse similar to modern-day yachting where redress could be granted and disqualification of the infringing vessel, and perhaps due to the nature of their defeat, *Cambria* did not lodge any protest or make any mention to the New York Yacht Club regatta committee. For decades after, this was a point debated in the yachting world with even the Vice President of the Yacht Racing Association, Lt-Colonel Sir George Leach, writing in *The Badminton Library of Sports and Pastimes*:

> The race was not a satisfactory one, as in the narrow waters she [the *Cambria*] was much hampered by other vessels, with one of which she came into collision, carrying away a fore-port shroud and fore-top-mast backstay, and springing the port arm of her fore-crosstrees. Later on, she also carried away her fore-topmast, losing all chance of even a good place. The race was won by the 'Magic,' a small schooner of 93 tons, the 'Cambria' being eighth, and the Cup therefore remained in the possession of the New York Yacht Club. Even if nothing had gone wrong with the 'Cambria,' pitted as she was against seventeen other vessels, her chance of winning the Cup would necessarily have been small.

With the first defence of America's Cup complete, the New York Yacht Club and its members felt vindicated in their decisions to race a fleet against a single challenger but were not deaf to the claims of unsporting behaviour. Immediately after the Cup races, the *Cambria* sailed up to Newport and took part in a number of club races whilst also firing up the competitive spirit amongst the owners by putting up a number of cups for races and challenges. Overall, the racing record of *Cambria* was poor that summer with the record showing just two wins and one of those by way of default when one fellow entrant the *Idler* suffered bob-stay damage.

However, what James Lloyd Ashbury achieved that summer was in similar vein to what the Stevens brothers and Colonel Hamilton achieved in the summer of 1851, namely a deepening of the ties between the Old and the New World and a deep respect for sporting and sportsmanlike endeavour. The American media were fascinated by this debonair, unmarried 40-year-old, blessed with a railway fortune and not immune to wearing his wealth with aplomb. *Vanity Fair* described him as:

> Singularly aristocratic in bearing, handsome in face, with a hand delicate as a woman's, set off by real diamonds of surpassing bigness, and with a name which able editors delighted to print in all newspapers, he made havoc as soon as he appeared. Yet such is his discretion that he has never been known to abuse the very general confidence which is believed to have been placed in him or to reveal to the world the romantic successes he has achieved. That he is still unmarried who is so favoured is less a reflection on himself than a reproach to the ladies who would be rejoiced to bear his name. For he is as tender-hearted as he is delicate, as impressionable as he is able, and would certainly make an excellent husband as he has made a statesman.

A mark of Ashbury's status was conferred by a visit of the then President of the United States, General Ulysses S. Grant for lunch onboard the *Cambria* before he left the country, already having commissioned Michael Ratsey of Cowes to build a new 265-ton challenger, the *Livonia* – named after a region of Russia (on the eastern shores of the Baltic now split between Latvia and Estonia) where Ashbury's railway company had provided track and rolling stock.

However, the *Livonia* challenge in 1871 was acrimonious from the start as Ashbury, smarting from what he saw as an unfair fleet racing against him in a game of chance, took on the New York Yacht Club, fighting fire with fire and riling the American club establishment with a multi-club challenge from all the clubs of which he was a member. What Ashbury was trying to avoid was another fleet race and, having built *Livonia*, he wanted success at all costs. Ahead of the contest, *The Times*, of 26 September 1871, featured a rather marvellous long letter written by someone who would only identify himself (in capitals) as AN ENGLISH YACHTSMAN (and we can only speculate who that might be), in support of Ashbury's stance:

> After considering the urgent representations of one of the donors – the only surviving one [George L. Schuyler], it appears of the cup, they decided that in all future contests for its possession, only vessel against vessel should be sent and not a whole fleet, as the club put forward to oppose the Cambria. This decision, so far as it affects the Livonia, reduces the contests to a dual character and, apart from the ordinary chances of match sailing, we consider that she has a reasonable chance of success. It is further satisfactory to note that the fate of the cup will

not be dependent upon one match, but that, to regain or retain possession of it, a majority in 11 matches must be won. The number of 11 matches was decided upon out of rather curious and irregular proceedings. Before it was decided that only one opposing vessel should be sent to meet the one challenging, Mr. Ashbury determined to take advantage of the wording of the Deed of Gift attached to the Cup and sent a separate and distinct challenge from each club that he is a member of – 12 in all.

Ultimately the challenge, Ashbury's last, failed with claims of 'unfair and unsportsmanlike proceedings'. Threats of sending *Livonia* back to England with back-and-forth communications proposing alternative formats for racing stirred in October 1871, before a final ultimatum from the New York Yacht Club ended the matter: 'The NYYC desire to be distinctly understood that they sail these races with you as the representative of the Royal Harwich YC only ...' Ashbury finally accepted this but the mystery of why he was so insistent on challenging under the flags of 12 clubs remains.

It was a fruitless episode, and the NYYC instructed a 'best of' seven races to be conducted in a final terse statement but then muddied the competition ahead of the first race bringing to the line two vessels – *Sappho* and *Columbia* – before the committee decided on the water which yacht would be better suited to the conditions to face the *Livonia*. More acrimony ensued through the first four races with race instructions being vague, marks being rounded incorrectly, protests lodged (that Ashbury claimed to have won), and then a final misunderstanding of first-to-four races rather than all seven races to be sailed. Ashbury tried to claim the America's Cup after sailing (and winning) private matches that he counted towards the Cup, but the New York Yacht Club ignored his requests.

'Unfair and unsportsmanlike proceedings' was a charge that the New York Yacht Club struggled to shake off and over the next 23 challenges, through to 1983, was an ever-present undercurrent in their running of the America's Cup. The 1871 races for the America's Cup also resulted in a significant cooling of the relationship between American and English yachtsmen and it was some 14 years (1885) before Great Britain once more challenged for the silver ewer.

Despite the travails and claims of 1871, and the subsequent returning of cups that Ashbury had donated to the club during his two challenges, what emerged was a clear resolution to the multi-boat defence tactic and greater fairness toward the challenging yacht. The New York Yacht Club still held many aces, as indeed the Defender, whoever that may be, does to this day through the uniqueness of the Deed of Gift governing the racing, but Ashbury's challenges laid a foundation that ultimately dictated the future course of the America's Cup forevermore.

On a private note, the challenge of 1870 had propelled Ashbury to the sort of social status in England that he felt was his birth right but was never fully embraced by the highest echelons. The 1871 challenge almost certainly put paid to any further recognition. He did however, sit for one term from 1874 through to 1880 in the Houses of Parliament as a Conservative politician, but upon the Liberals regaining control of the Brighton seats in 1880, he disappeared from public life completely and was never again seen in yachting circles.

A series of poor investments and divestments, of note the Merrivale sheep station in Otautau, on the South Island of New Zealand, which in a census on the 31 May 1885 had some 19,506 sheep, became a huge financial liability. This saw Ashbury relentlessly in creditor court fighting to stave off bankruptcy, and it ultimately led to his demise. Fifteen years later, on 3 September 1895, he was found dead at his London house having seemingly taken an overdose, reportedly of the high-strength opiate and cannabis-based narcotic Chlorodyne. He was described unflatteringly by some in the tabloid journals as being a 'gentleman of no occupation'.

Ashbury's Last Will & Testament, updated and dated before his death in 1895, showed the enormous pressure that he was under, cutting out completely from his Will his fellow partners in the Merrivale venture. Still believing himself to be a man of means, he bequeathed huge sums (£500) to named associates and even remarked right at the end that, 'I request the executors to see that the hearse has not more than two horses nor must there be more than one mourning coach with one or two horses.' His death certificate, dated 3 September 1895 showed a 'Gross Value of Personal Estate' to be just £400.

The Times was matter of fact, saying in their obituary column of 11 September 1895:

> The death is announced as having taken place suddenly on the 3rd September of Mr. James Lloyd Ashbury, formerly one of the members of Parliament for Brighton. Mr. Ashbury first contested Brighton as a Conservative in the election of November 1868, there being on that

occasion three Liberal candidates, one of whom was Mr. Fawcett, and two Conservative candidates. Mr. Ashbury failed on this occasion to secure a seat, but in the election of February 1874, he was returned at the head of the poll, with Major-General Shute as his colleague, Mr. White and Mr. Fawcett, the two Liberals, being ousted from the representation. In the election of 1880, however, Mr. Ashbury failed to retain his seat.

A 'Statesman' profile that had appeared in *Vanity Fair* in October 1874, alongside a famous line-drawing of Ashbury with his incredibly thick ginger beard, summed up well his life and career and is where the story of this first challenger for the America's Cup should end:

> Mr Ashbury is a man of extraordinary aspirations. Started in life by his father as a worker in the family railway carriage works, he gained his first views of the world from the making of patent axles and the fitting of rolling stock. At one-and-twenty he was promoted to be a manager of the concern and before he was thirty, he had become possessed of the chief interest in it. But being then as he has remained to this day, moved by intense energy, and impressed with the knowledge of his own powers he soon became aware that the career of mere industry was far too restricted to offer any promise of conveying to the world at large a due sense of the great qualities he felt within himself. At four-and-forty therefore he resolved to fit himself for higher things by becoming for a time a sailor and a man of pleasure, so he bought a yacht and importing into his new pursuits that strict attention to business which he had learned in early youth. He competed in successive regatta's until at last, he won the ocean race to America and raised a quarrel with the New York Yacht Club the merits of which the most lavish expenditure of print paper has left the present time in indecision ... Even now he has risen so far as to excite that fear, which is the tribute first paid to worth, and the Royal Yacht Squadron, not daring to face the companionship and comparison of Mr Ashbury with its members, shut against him the portals which it was felt he should command and thus earned for itself eternal regret and repentance.

The America's Cup, so often portrayed subsequently as the poisoned chalice of international sports, thus began. Its history is long and storied with those who tried and failed, who came close, who lapped at the flames, whose lives have been either made or broken by the sheer desperation to win at all costs. It was Ashbury's challenges that ultimately laid the ultra-competitive groundwork for vociferous and tenacious defences of the America's Cup forevermore. The New York Yacht Club developed an iron will and resolve to defend the trophy almost at any cost through the golden era of the J Class in the early 20th century and on to the modern-day challenges in the 12-Metre class after the Second World War, although challenged with almost bottomless pits of money and will to succeed by the likes of Sir Thomas Lipton and Sir T.O.M. Sopwith. Ultimately the club lost the trophy in 1983, succumbing perhaps to the inevitable, but fighting tooth and nail to the end. They have never seen it since.

The America's Cup is a unique regatta by dint of its curious construction and its protection by the statute of law so rigorously upheld in the New York courthouses. Despite numerous challenges to the Deed of Gift, subsequent re-writes and amendments, it is still today in an unequivocal position at the very apex of the sailing and sporting world.

But to proffer the last word, it's rather fitting to end with the great sportswriter Tom Callahan of *The Washington Post* who spoke most eloquently on the trophy and event saying: 'The America's Cup, yachting's great and garish grail, is a tumorous tureen no handsomer than a camel.'

Quite.

Te Rehutai, the winner of the America's Cup in 2021.

POSTSCRIPT

At the point where I leave this book, James Lloyd Ashbury's second challenge in 1871 had resulted in failure, but the history of the America's Cup had really only just begun. However, the importance of the context in which the race came into being, with the conjunction of Victorian Britain and an increasingly assertive New World, has hopefully been demonstrated.

Through multiple eras of yacht design, the Cup itself has lasted through the American Civil War, two World Wars, global financial calamities, a pandemic even, but has come through to triumph as the trophy that epitomises the very pinnacle of yachting. The New York Yacht Club held on to the ewer for 132 years, bending the rules, withholding technology, sailing brilliantly and designing superbly, until the Australians in 1983 brought everything together in one competitive package and trumped the Americans in their own backyard.

This extraordinary victory kick-started the modern-day America's Cup and placed design at the centre of every campaign since. It also highlighted a new professionalism, arguably first brought in by the great Dennis Conner in 1980, creating an event where the mantra, 'There is no second', is just as relevant today and seeps into every competitor, owner, designer and team member. The evolution to boats that foil above the water at speeds unimaginable 20 years ago is leading a global trend, a movement that is ever-present even down to the grass-roots club level.

The yachts of the current America's Cup, the AC75s, are the gold standard of the yachting world that define the sport. The incoming challengers have brought Formula 1 teams, data scientists, mechanical engineers, physicists, and every advance in computational and simulation excellence, all to produce ultimately the fastest boat. It is today, as it ever was, a crucible in which mankind's greatest technical thinking is played out.

As much as I appreciate the technology, one immutable factor remains and that is the human side of the America's Cup. Go back through the history, and even into the modern day and you find incredible personal rivalries that run deep and crystallise in the white-hot heat of battle for supremacy: Vanderbilt against Sopwith, Lipton against Morgan, Osgood against Ashbury, Iselin against Dunraven, Turner against Bond, Conner against Blackaller, Coutts against Conner, Burling against Spithill ... the list goes on and will continue forevermore. Within these rivalries, the character of those individuals enormously embellish the Cup, its legend and continual fascination. The human element is, I would argue, as important as the technology, and it is the element that unites support, elicits tales to be told and ultimately decides the Cup's fate.

My enthusiasm for the America's Cup, an enthusiasm shared by many hundreds of thousands of fans around the world, is reaffirmed with every edition. Just when you think you have seen it all, it wriggles and writhes to another level of technical astonishment and wonder, whilst the trophy itself remains a shining beacon of Victoriana: an unchanging, ugly-beauty with its myriad of mis-quotes and fancy that draws in the hopeful, like the Sirens singing on the flowery shores of the Aegean. Its allure has been described to me as being almost holy, and when it's near, I have felt the reverence that springs from a lifetime of wonder at something that captivates and enthrals in equal measure.

Having the opportunity to delve as deeply as I have done during the research of this book has been a pleasure, and it is my true hope that it enlightens and inspires you to find out more. My belief is that the America's Cup is the greatest sporting trophy that mankind has ever created – and to that I raise a glass of deep respect to the Marquess of Anglesey, Lord Wilton and the Royal Yacht Squadron, John Cox Stevens, George Lee Schuyler and the New York Yacht Club, not to mention the yacht *America* herself, and all those involved in that first race for the creation of such a magnificent contest 'making it perpetually a challenge cup for friendly competition between foreign countries' where: 'There is no second'.

The America's Cup in Jeddah, Saudi Arabia, for the November 2023 Preliminary Regatta.

THERE IS NO SECOND – THE CAST LIST

(In order of appearance)

The British

Marquess of Anglesey	Purchaser in 1848 of the silver ewer that would become 'America's Cup'
Duke of Cumberland	Instigator of the Cumberland Society (1775) sponsoring Thames yacht racing
Lord Grantham	Chairman of the first meeting to form The Yacht Club at 'The Thatch'd', St James's
Lord Yarborough	First Commodore of the RYS
Marquess of Donegall	Controversial Commodore of the RYS
Earl of Wilton	The steadying hand as Commodore of the RYS
Queen Victoria	Queen of England who extends a hand of friendship to the Americans
Prince Albert	Queen Victoria's husband and instigator of the Great Exhibition in 1851
Henry Bulwer	British Ambassador to the US who tipped-off the Earl of Wilton about the yacht *America*
John Mellin	Yeoman of the Signals on HMY *Victoria & Albert*
Henry Wickham	Yeoman of the Signals on HMY *Victoria & Albert*
Robert Stephenson	Owner of *Titania*, the only yacht to accept the challenge of *America* after the race in 1851
John de Blaquiere	Purchaser of *America* after the win in 1851
James Lloyd Ashbury	First British challenger for America's Cup in 1870

The Americans

John Cox Stevens	First Commodore of the NYYC
Edwin Augustus Stevens	Syndicate owner of the yacht *America*
George L. Schuyler	Author of the original 'Deed of Gift' in 1857
Alexander Hamilton	Syndicate owner of the yacht *America*
Hamilton Wilkes	First Vice Commodore of the NYYC and syndicate owner of the yacht *America*
John K. Beekman Finlay	Syndicate owner of the yacht *America*
Captain Richard Brown	Helmsman of the yacht *America* in 1851, nicknamed 'Old Dick'
Nelson Comstock	First mate on the yacht *America*
James Gordon Bennett Jnr.	Owner of the New York Herald and the yacht *Dauntless*

Designers and Builders

Philip Sainty	Talented boatbuilder jailed on smuggling charges, release secured by Marquess of Anglesey
John Scott Russell	Scottish author of the wave-line theory
George Steers	Designer of the *America*, mistakenly credited on the America's Cup trophy as the 'builder'
Reuben Howland Wilson	American sailmaker and designer of *America*'s flat-cut sails
William H. Brown	New York-based master builder of the yacht *America*
George Rogers Ratsey	British sailmaker based in Cowes
Michael Ratsey of Cowes	Builder of *Aurora*, *Cambria* and *Livonia*
Joseph White of Cowes	Master boatbuilder

The Yachts

Pearl	Built by Philip Sainty following release from jail, owned by the Marquess of Anglesey
Waterwitch	Built by Joseph White, first owned by Lord Belfast, later the Marquess of Donegall
Maria	Built by Robert L. Stevens, brother of John C. Stevens, reputed to be the fastest yacht of its time
Mary Taylor	A pilot built designed by designer George Steers, precursor of *America*
Gimcrack	The schooner, designed by Steers, where the NYYC first met and formed its constitution in 1844
America	The triumphant New World winner of the 1851 'RYS £100 Cup', first owned by NYYC syndicate
Laverock	British cutter beaten in an impromptu race when *America* first arrived in the Solent
Wildfire	Unofficial entrant to the 1851 race, which could have actually beaten *America* across the finish line
Titania	Loses against *America* following the RYS £100 Cup race in 1851
Alarm	One of the fastest yachts in the British fleet, stands by while *Arrow* runs aground in the 1851 race
Arrow	A yacht with a stellar pedigree in Solent races, runs aground during the 1851 race
Aurora	Likely to have finished far closer to the *America* in 1851 than has been appreciated
Cambria	Wins the Atlantic Yacht Race of 1870 but loses Ashbury's first challenge for America's Cup
Dauntless	Loses to *Cambria* in the Atlantic Yacht Race
Livonia	Commissioned by James Lloyd Ashbury for his second unsuccessful challenge for America's Cup

Illustration and photographic credits

Plates	Ref No	Credit
i	1	Ben Wood / PPL
	2	Shutterstock
ii	3	The London Illustrated News
	4	Bridgeman Images
	5	East Cowes Heritage Centre
	6	Bridgeman Images
iii	7	Reproduced by permission of Chatsworth Settlement Trustees
	8	Reproduced by permission of Chatsworth Settlement Trustees
iv	9	Shutterstock
	10	Shutterstock
v	11	Bob Fisher Archive / PPL
	12	Bob Fisher Archive / PPL
	13	Bob Fisher Archive / PPL
vi	14	Ben Wood / PPL
	15	Bob Fisher Archive / PPL
	16	Alamy
vii	17	Bridgeman Images
	18	Bob Fisher Archive / PPL
viii	19	Carlo Borlenghi / America's Cup Archive
	20	Alamy
ix	21	Ben Wood / PPL
	22	Ben Wood / PPL
x	23	Ben Wood / PPL
	24	Bob Fisher Archive / PPL
xi	25	Ben Wood / PPL
	26	Ben Wood / PPL
xii	27	Ben Wood / PPL
	28	Ben Wood / PPL
xiii	29	Ben Wood / PPL
	30	Bob Fisher Archive / PPL
xiv	31	Ben Wood / PPL
	32	Ian Dear Archive / PPL
	33	Bob Fisher Archive / PPL
xv	34	Bob Fisher Archive / PPL
	35	Alamy
xvi	36	Bob Fisher Archive / PPL
	37	Ian Dear Archive / PPL
	38	Bob Fisher Archive / PPL
	39	Principal Probate Office

Chapter openings – illustration and photographic credits

Page 16	Alamy
Page 32	Shutterstock
Page 48	Shutterstock
Page 64	Painting by Steven Dews, courtesy of Rosenstiels
Page 80	Ben Wood / PPL
Page 100	Alamy
Page 116	Ben Wood / PPL
Page 130	Bob Fisher Archive / PPL
Page 146	Bob Fisher Archive / PPL
Page 160	Ben Wood / PPL / Vanity Fair

ACKNOWLEDGEMENTS

My deepest thanks go to the following for There is no second: Grant Dalton for giving me the inspiration, encouragement and most of all, trust. Hamish Hooper and Ryan Pellett at Emirates Team New Zealand for their unwavering support and assistance in curating and creating the book. Ben Wood at Island Images for his dogged determination in project managing the production and photography. Nicola Kearton for her outstanding proof reading and sensitive editing of the original text. Brian Cantwell for his peerless typesetting skills and wise commercial words. Barry Pickthall at PPL Media Library for his jovial support of my writing and for access to his remarkable marine library. Julie Crocker at the Royal Archives for building a pathway through the gloom of research and James Cronan at the National Archives for providing the light at the end of the tunnel. Yachting journalist and author Adrian Morgan for his immediate support on the research. Danny Watson and all the team at the Royal Victoria Yacht Club for access to the Club's wonderful memorabilia. Finally I'd like to thank the marine artist Steven Dews for his outstanding and truthful painting of *America* in 1851 which we are honoured to be using on the front cover.

Thank you all.